# On Pestilence

T0385865

# On Pestilence

*A Renaissance Treatise on Plague*

Girolamo Mercuriale

Translated and with an Introduction by Craig Martin

**PENN**

UNIVERSITY OF PENNSYLVANIA PRESS

PHILADELPHIA

Cures and remedies described in this book
are presented for historical purposes only and
should not be used as medical treatments.

Published by
University of Pennsylvania Press
Philadelphia, Pennsylvania 19104-4112
www.upenn.edu/pennpress

Printed in the United States of America on acid-free paper
10 9 8 7 6 5 4 3 2 1

A catalogue record for this book is available
from the Library of Congress.
ISBN 978-0-8122-5354-2

*In memory of Russell Martin*

# CONTENTS

# Introduction

## The Plague in Venice and Girolamo Mercuriale's Medical Theory and Practice

Plague struck much of northern Italy and Sicily from 1575 to 1578. It was perhaps the most significant epidemic to afflict Italy and especially Venice since the fourteenth century.[1] Between a third and a quarter of Venice's population died. The plague transformed the city's civic rituals and architectural tradition. Construction soon began on the Church of the Redentore, designed by Andrea Palladio, and the city inaugurated the *Festa del Redentore* (the Feast of the Redeemer) to celebrate the end of the plague, which is still commemorated every July with a procession and fireworks.[2] The epidemic sparked an unparalleled wave of publications that narrated the unfolding of the calamity. These writings proposed explanations and remedies, as governments and populaces sought solace and protection from the disease.[3] Both university-trained physicians and laymen took up the task of writing these accounts.

Among those treatises written by learned elites, Girolamo Mercuriale's *On Pestilence* (1577) holds a notorious position in the history of medicine and epidemic disease. A number of Mercuriale's contemporaries blamed him for misdiagnosing the plague and demanding the removal of the quarantine at Venice, a demand that Venice's rulers met. His detractors believed his actions caused the deaths of tens of thousands of Venetians. Mercuriale's perceived role in exacerbating the epidemic that devastated Venice's population is central to the treatise's arguments and the controversies that surrounded its publication. Recent scholarship has largely interpreted the treatise as an attempt to safeguard or revive his reputation and career, a career that had been up to this point spectacular.[4]

By 1577, Mercuriale had already developed an international reputation and a long history with Venice. A native of Forlì, in the Papal States, he took his medical degree from the College of Physicians of Venice in 1555. In 1562, he went to Rome, where he served as physician to Alessandro Farnese, a cardinal and

great patron of the arts. Much of his early educational and professional life cir-
cled around Venice and Padua, where he studied and collaborated with Vittore
Trincavelli, a professor of practical medicine; with Gabriele Falloppio, who is
best known for anatomical investigations; and with Melchiorre Guilandino
(Wieland), who became prefect of the university's Orto Botanico (Botanic Gar-
den) and professor of pharmacological substances (known as "simples"). In 1569,
Mercuriale was appointed ordinary professor in practical medicine at Padua.[5]
In his first years there, he published an extensive, highly regarded work on cuta-
neous diseases and bodily excrement; and he treated the Holy Roman Emperor
Maximilian II, for which he was awarded the title of Count Palatine.[6]

    If the goal of the treatise was to stabilize or even enhance his reputation,
it likely succeeded. Despite discontent with his failure to diagnose the plague
in Venice and Padua, Mercuriale remained a professor of medicine for nearly
twenty-five more years, earning one of the highest salaries for his profession in
all of Italy. He left Padua for the University of Bologna in 1587, accepting a lofty
annual salary of 1,200 *scudi,* honorary citizenship, and an exemption from taxes.[7]
Five years later he took up a position at Pisa, where he was paid 2,000 *scudi* a
year. He innovated in the fields of gynecology, pediatrics, and toxicology, publishing numerous textbooks.[8] He was regarded as being among the most important physicians and professors of medicine in Europe until his death in 1606.[9]

    Mercuriale's advice to the Venetian government illustrates the dynamics of
medical expertise in sixteenth-century Italy. The episode provides an example
of experts' inability to agree and of a divided government that opted for the
advice of a prominent, well-connected physician over the recommendations of
a government body, the Health Office (*Provveditori alla Sanità*), that was com-
missioned to protect Venetians' lives. *On Pestilence* offers slightly hidden justi-
fications and rationales, if not rationalizations, for Mercuriale's diagnosis, yet
its historical significance does not end there. Mercuriale put forward a deeply
learned understanding of plague that employed historical analyses of epidemics
and made extensive recommendations for public health measures, a relative novelty for plague treatises. While some writers of plague treatises, like Girolamo
Manfredi (1430–1493), wrote short chapters containing advice for the prevention of the disease in cities, many did not consider the question.[10] For example,
John of Burgundy's plague treatise, among the most widely circulated during the
late Middle Ages, contains no historical analysis or advice for cities. Sixteenth-
century English adaptions of it emphasized religious elements above all else.[11]
Neither the leading Florentine physician Tommaso Del Garbo (1305–1370) nor
Marsilio Ficino (1433–1499), one of the most famous Renaissance humanists,

Figure 1. A portrait of Mercuriale by Theodor de Bry (1528–1598). The engraving identifies Mercuriale as professor at Padua, and the caption reads: "The sun and phoenix of physicians, Girolamo Mercuriale was graced with this face." Courtesy of the Wellcome Collections (https://creativecommons.org/licenses/by/4.0/).

discussed these topics in their plague treatises, which were reprinted throughout the sixteenth century.[12] Raymond Chalin de Vinario, active toward the end of fourteenth century, passed over public health but included a short astrologically minded history of the plague that started with the planetary conjunctions of 1345 and ended in 1382.[13] French plague treatises, which grew significantly in number after 1580, show little to no concern with dissecting past plagues.[14]

Mercuriale was able to make more thorough historical comparisons than fourteenth- and fifteenth-century authors, in part, because he had access to a greater number of relevant primary sources, especially the writings of ancient Greek historians. Their works only began to circulate broadly in western Europe around the turn of the sixteenth century. Lorenzo Valla first translated Thucydides' *History of the Peloponnesian War*, with its description of the Athenian plague (430–426 BCE), into Latin in 1452, and it was not printed until 1483.[15] Procopius' *The Persian War*, in which he described the Justinianic plague that began in 541 CE, was not available in print in Latin until 1509.[16] The Latin rendition of Evagrius, an ecclesiastical historian who witnessed epidemics of the sixth century, came out in 1544.[17] Even some Latin works, such as Lucretius' *On the Nature of Things*, gained greater currency with physicians only at the beginning of the sixteenth century.[18] Although Georg Agricola (1494–1555)—a physician, philologist, and expert on minerals and mining—briefly touched upon many plagues of antiquity in his own plague treatise, the only references to the Justinianic plague were based not on Greek sources but on Gregory of Tours (538–594 CE), who wrote in Latin.[19]

The craft of history underwent significant changes in the first half of the sixteenth century. Scholars increasingly used critical and comparative techniques to judge the reliability of ancient and later writings while distancing themselves from medieval understandings of the past. As Anthony Grafton writes, "By 1560, both in Italy and in the north, a new *ars historica* had taken shape."[20] Mercuriale honed his critical acumen on these newly available sources, contending that in order to classify and diagnose epidemics it was necessary to compare them to outbreaks of the past. Accordingly, he mined a broad range of ancient, medieval, and contemporary writings, bolstered by his own experiences, in an effort to understand the disaster that afflicted northern Italy. As a whole, the treatise is emblematic of Renaissance medical humanism, which employed comparative history and philology in its practice and theory. Mercuriale sought to redefine the concept of plague according to his reading of the Hippocratic *Epidemics*, while simultaneously putting forward a historical account of pestilences dependent on a panoply of descriptions of ancient epidemics, including the plague of

Athens, the Antonine plague, the Justinianic plague and subsequent epidemics in the Byzantine Empire, and the medieval plagues that began in Europe in 1347 and continued throughout the early modern period.

## Venice's Plague of 1575–1577

In the three centuries that followed the plague's reentry into western Europe in 1347, epidemics with high rates of mortality recurred with varying frequency and virulence. Laboratory analysis, including that based on DNA harvested from mass graves, has shown that the bubonic plague, the disease caused by *Yersinia pestis*, a bacterium typically carried by fleas that live on rats and other rodents, was responsible for three extended pandemics.[21] The earliest, the Justinianic plague, struck the Eastern Roman Empire in 541 CE and resurfaced seventeen times in the next 210 years, according to one historian's count.[22] The second plague pandemic began in the middle of the fourteenth century and lasted until the eighteenth. Its first wave in western Europe from 1347 to 1353 is often referred to as the Black Death. The modern outbreak began in China in the latter part of the nineteenth century. It was not until 1894, in the third pandemic, that Kitasato Shibasaburō and Alexandre Yersin isolated the plague bacillus.[23]

Symptoms of bubonic plague include high fever and inflammation of lymph nodes that lead to swelling and the formation of buboes, infected welts or tumors, typically on the groin, armpits, and neck. The plague takes its name from these buboes. Additionally, smaller sores and pustules appear on many who are infected. While antibiotics can now cure the disease, it is often fatal when left untreated. Although bubonic plague spreads primarily through the rat flea (*Xenopsylla cheopis*), recent research has pointed to other possible vectors, including the human flea (*Pulex irritans*) and lice.[24] Septicemic plague can be contracted through small cuts and abrasions when touching or skinning dead animals or through the ingestion of diseased meat. Michelle Ziegler emphasizes that septicemic plague is likely under-diagnosed now, which she says is "a reminder that we need to be cautious when we use medieval data."[25] If the disease develops into a pneumonic plague, a particularly deadly form that has been diagnosed in the Congo, Uganda, India, and China in recent years, it can be spread through inhalation, especially in crowded, cool, wet environments.[26] It is possible that the plague of Venice did not spread in the pneumonic form.[27]

In premodern times, large portions of populations were affected by the disease and died. Some have estimated that the Black Death killed half of the population of western Europe.[28] After the first wave of plague in the fourteenth century, European cities experienced epidemic disease regularly. Tuscan cities, for example, suffered from severe epidemics at least nine different times from 1348 to 1430.[29] Many of these later epidemics were more localized than the initial plague, affecting only specific cities or regions. During the Renaissance, plague visited Venice in 1478, 1528, and 1555; the outbreak of 1575–1577 was extremely lethal, killing over 50,000 people out of a total population between 160,000 and 190,000.[30] In nearby Padua, a much smaller city that was part of the territory of the Republic of Venice, over 10,000 people died.[31]

Venice's plague of 1575–1577 was part of an epidemic that spread throughout the Italian peninsula and beyond. The plague had appeared in Trent and Sicily in May of 1575 and arrived in Venice by July of that year. Nearly four thousand people died in a first wave that lasted until the winter, when the deaths subsided. By late spring of 1576, few deaths were reported, but at the beginning of June of 1576 the number of deaths increased, prompting thousands to evacuate the city and the Health Office to enact quarantines.[32]

Quarantines in Venice during the sixteenth century entailed large-scale surveillance and intervention. The Health Office inspected those entering the city on suspicious ships, often those arriving from cities known to be suffering from plague. They also looked for Venetians with symptoms. The homes of those who died were shuttered, emptied, and cleaned. Anyone who had been in a condemned house was quarantined for eight days. Households suspected of harboring individuals exposed to plague were closed up for fourteen or twenty-two days. Many merchants arriving in the city were quarantined with their goods on the Lazzaretto Nuovo, a small island in the Venetian lagoon, together with convalescing patients. Employing threats of force, city officials brought the bodies of the dead and the individuals suffering the worst cases—many of whom were described as poor—to the Lazzaretto Vecchio. Dogs and cats were exterminated. Some Venetians who were described as being from the lower classes were reported as trying to hide their disease, partly because they feared the Health Office would incinerate their possessions, partly because they were scared of dying in the lazaretto.[33]

Much of the population hated the quarantine, and the Venetian government grew concerned about its economic and political repercussions. Leaders worried that the loss of tax revenue caused by the ban of goods entering the city might weaken the republic's defenses.[34] A number of physicians from both Venice and Padua, including Mercuriale, were called to debate the cause of the disease before the doge and other dignitaries. The question at hand was whether the disease was "true plague" (*vera pestis* in Latin, *vera peste* in the vernacular) as the Health

Office maintained. The other possibilities were that it was a less contagious disease, such as what was called pestilential or malign fever, or a less dangerous yet still communicable disease referred to as "contagious disease" (*mal contagioso* or *morbo contagioso*). The definition and means for diagnosing "true plague," a term that does not precisely correspond with modern medical categories, were subject to debate. The physicians of the Health Office preferred to look at symptoms, such as buboes and carbuncles, while Mercuriale forged a different path, concentrating on the cause, diffusion, and lethality of the disease. Similar debates about identifying "true plague" spread throughout Italy in these years, becoming a prominent feature of plague writings.[35]

At Venice, the physicians presented a range of views in front of the doge. Some endorsed the diagnosis of "true plague," others posited that it was not plague but that it might escalate into "true plague," and others declared that it was simply not plague at all. Mercuriale's view corresponded with the last position, as he and Girolamo Capodivacca, his colleague at Padua, argued that the quarantine should be lifted. They offered to treat personally the sick on the condition that the government publicly declare that there was no plague in Venice and lift many of the restrictions intended to limit the spread of the disease.[36] The Venetian government accepted, against the wishes of the Health Office. According to a contemporary account, the doge, Alvise I Mocenigo, applauded the professors from Padua.[37] The official historian of Venice, Andrea Morosini (1558–1618), wrote that the Venetian populace rejoiced.[38] Mercuriale and Capodivacca, along with two surgeons, four Venetian physicians, and two Jesuit priests, treated patients, and their assistants lanced boils and let blood.[39]

As public health measures were lifted and Mercuriale and his companions visited patients, the number of deaths increased throughout June. One of the Jesuits accompanying Mercuriale died. The other priest along with one of the surgeons became gravely ill.[40] At the end of the month, Mercuriale and Capodivacca requested to return to Padua. Waiting in quarantine in Venice, the two physicians wrote a defense of their diagnosis, while others present in Venice, including the ambassador of Florence, blamed them for spreading the disease and for the rise in deaths. Mercuriale returned to Padua in July, where he found the university closed.[41] The Venetian government reimposed the quarantine, which strained the city's resources as hospitals filled. By November, many of the sites were at or beyond capacity, and new plans were made to incinerate goods suspected of harboring infection rather than disinfect them by exposing them to the open air.[42]

After the outbreak temporarily died down with the arrival of winter, the university reopened in January of 1577, and Mercuriale began his lectures on the plague. The lectures presented a shifted position, as he agreed that the epidemic became "true plague," but not until July and August of 1576, after he had already left Venice. Girolamo Zacco, a Paduan physician who had studied at the university, recorded the lectures and saw to their publication.[43] That spring, the plague returned to Venice, killing approximately another four thousand people, before being officially declared over in July 1577.[44]

## The University of Padua and Medical Humanism

The University of Padua was perhaps the most renowned school of medicine in Europe in the sixteenth century. Its innovative and hands-on approach to teaching clinical medicine, anatomy, and pharmacology attracted students from all of Italy, northern Europe, and the Venetian Empire's eastern possessions. The Venetian senate controlled both the city of Padua and its university, taking great steps to ensure that it brought fame and glory to the republic. Although instruction privileged direct experience with patients, bodies, and treatments, the professoriate at Padua were also leaders in the medical humanism that characterized much of elite medicine during the Renaissance.[45]

Mercuriale embraced both aspects of the Paduan tradition. He directly observed patients, emphasizing experience. But his engagement with the tradition of medical humanism stands out. Medical humanism was a cultural and intellectual movement that sought to recover, interrogate, and appropriate ancient medical writings. This movement, tied to Renaissance humanism more broadly, began in the second half of the fifteenth century. Theodore Gaza (c. 1398–c. 1475) and Niccolò Leoniceno (1428–1524), among others, sought to correct the Latin translations of the Aristotelian *Problems* and Galen's writings that they believed were marred by scribal errors and infelicitous scholastic phrasings. Improving the accuracy of these texts, which were widely used to train physicians, was seen to be not merely an academic exercise but an activity that could save lives. Mistranslations of cures and medical theory risked patients' health.[46]

Throughout the sixteenth century, scholars and physicians followed Gaza's and Leoniceno's lead. The corpus of Greek medical writings expanded as Hippocrates' and Galen's complete works were edited, printed, and translated into Latin.[47] Mercuriale participated in these projects. *On Pestilence* reflects his investigations into Hippocratic works that had been largely unavailable during the Middle Ages, such as several books of the *Epidemics* and Galen's commentary on them, and even into a few Renaissance fabrications, such as a commentary on *Humors* that was falsely attributed to Galen.[48] Later in his career, Mercuriale lectured on and wrote a commentary on the *Epidemics*, a sign of his continued interest in the text.[49] Medical humanists, however, investigated far more than just the writings of Hippocrates and Galen. The number of ancient medical authorities grew as Oribasius, Aëtius, Dioscorides, and Celsus became widely available in print. Medical writings from the Islamicate world by Averroes, Avicenna, Rhazes, Avenzoar, and Albucasis that had helped form medieval curricula were edited, retranslated, and reprinted according to standards similar to those that had been devised for Greek authors.[50]

Mercuriale, like many proponents of medical humanism, understood his investigation into medical writings of the past to be part of the larger culture of humanism and historical investigation. In his eyes, interpreting Galen and Hippocrates required general inquiry into the past. Some of his earliest printed works reflected this conviction. In 1569, he published *On the Art of Gymnastics*, an exposition of the activities and exercises practiced in ancient Roman gymnasiums (*palaestrae*) and baths, which was based on a rich reading of ancient sources and on his collaboration with Pirro Ligorio, a trailblazer in antiquarian and archeological research.[51]

Well before the plague arrived in 1575, Mercuriale analyzed ancient medical and historical writings on epidemic disease. In his *Various Lectures* (1570), a collection of mainly philological notes, he compared the accounts of the plague of Athens found in Hippocratic works, Thucydides, and Lucretius. Mercuriale concluded that the Hippocratic *On Breaths* and Lucretius' *On the Nature of Things* agreed on the aerial nature of plague because, in his view, Hippocrates was a disciple of Democritus and Epicurean atomism traces back to Democritus. Thus, according to Mercuriale, Hippocrates called Democritus' atoms miasmas, and Lucretius preferred to call them seeds.[52] Later on in the work, Mercuriale proposed an emendation to Plutarch's discussion of animal and meteorological signs of future plagues.[53] In *On Pestilence*, Mercuriale's antiquarian and historical interests resurfaced, as he analyzed plagues described by Hippocrates, Galen, and their contemporaries as well as historical accounts of the Justinianic plague, of the medieval plague, and of recent ones.

While it was a shibboleth of some proponents of medical humanism that they were combatting the barbarism of Arabic-writing authors in an attempt to purify the field of medicine, Mercuriale's approach to the Islamicate medieval tradition in *On Pestilence* was largely conciliatory. At times, he grouped together classical authors and medical theorists who wrote in Arabic, referring to them as the "ancients" (*veteres*), a term that conferred authority. He repeatedly cited

Avicenna (Ibn Sīnā), whose *Canon* was the subject of numerous medieval commentaries and remained a fixture as a textbook in northern Italy throughout the sixteenth century.[54]

In addition to older writings, several Renaissance medical theorists influenced Mercuriale. The most important ones were Jean Fernel (1497–1558) and Girolamo Fracastoro (1476 or 1478–1553). Fernel, a French physician, developed a theory of occult causes that explained certain diseases as being caused by hidden qualities. The etiology of these diseases is analogous to the workings of poisons that produce powerful effects that cannot be easily explained through manifest qualities (hot, cold, wet, dry) but are known only through experience.[55] Fracastoro, a physician from Verona who had ties to the University of Padua, contended that the contagious nature of diseases are the result of sympathy and putrefaction transmitted through seeds.[56] While Mercuriale was influenced by these two thinkers, he was also highly critical of certain aspects of their theories, and his adoption of their ideas was hesitant and incomplete.

The multiple and wide-ranging sources that Mercuriale employed might suggest an unfettered eclecticism, yet his historical, medical, and theoretical investigations are indicative of his desire to gain as much information as possible about the nature of epidemic disease. He proposed a common etiology for plagues and therefore believed that the characteristics and course of the disease could be grasped through historical research. Mining histories and past medical writings was the best means to establish the causes of plague and appropriate responses to it.

## Mercuriale's *On Pestilence*

During and immediately after the plague of 1575–1578, printed pamphlets and treatises that discussed the epidemic flooded Italy's book market. Many narrated the development of the disaster, describing the plague's arrival, its spread, governmental and popular reaction, and the suffering endured. Physicians included similar narrations in their treatises before embarking on discussions of causes and treatment. For the most part, the authors of these treatises emphasized contagion between humans as the main factor in the plague's spread. They often minimized the role of the stars and of the air, which had been mainstays of earlier theories of plagues.[57] Mercuriale, however, endorsed the air's primary role in causing plague. Many treatises were explicitly critical of Mercuriale's theories and actions in Venice. For example, Girolamo Donzellini, a physician trained at Padua, had been freed from jail in Venice, where he had been held on charges of heresy, to treat the sick during the plague. In a treatise printed in 1577, he defended the Health Office's diagnosis based on bodily symptoms such as buboes and criticized those, like Mercuriale, who denied it was "true plague."[58] Similarly, an astrologer from Verona, named Annibale Raimondo, dismissed air as a cause and blamed contamination of Venice's wells with sea water for the disease.[59] Mercuriale's treatise defended his views against such charges.

The most obvious model for Mercuriale's treatise was Giovanni Filippo Ingrassia's *Communication on the Pestiferous and Contagious Disease*, an account of the plague in Sicily printed in 1576.[60] Ingrassia (1510–1580) had studied and worked in northern Italy and Naples, where he wrote on Galen and treated aristocratic patients.[61] In 1563, he was appointed the *protomedico* of Sicily, making him responsible for the public health of the island, a position he continued to hold when the plague struck in 1575. Like Ingrassia, Mercuriale narrated the chronological unfolding of the disease; diagnosed it, determining whether it was "true plague" or not; offered advice to governments on how to combat the spread of the disease; and recommended treatments. While plague treatises represent a thriving genre dating back to the fourteenth century, Mercuriale's and Ingrassia's treatises exhibit novel approaches. Unlike most earlier treatises, theirs included detailed narratives of recent events. Furthermore, in comparison to many of their immediate predecessors in Italy, they devoted relatively greater attention to public health measures, a sign of the increasingly important role that physicians played in advising governments.[62]

Much of the advice that physicians gave to governments depended on determining whether an outbreak was "true plague" or another less dangerous disease. Accordingly, Mercuriale's treatise devoted significant attention to this question as he slightly altered his analysis of the disease from what he had argued before the doge in June of 1576. In his lectures, he accepted that plague was contagious, spreading from person to person, and that, indeed, at least by the end of the summer of 1576, the epidemic raging in Venice was "true plague." While many of Mercuriale's contemporaries, including those working for Venice's Health Office, relied on symptoms to diagnose plague, Mercuriale maintained that the disease was defined by its lethality and rapid spread. Therefore, "true plague" must be widespread and kill quickly. Its epidemiological profile is the true sign. On a practical level, this definition presented a paradox. Adhering to Mercuriale's theory means that alarms for "true plague" are to be sounded only after many deaths. As a result, governments that follow this line of thinking cannot implement preventative measures before the disease becomes widespread and considered "true plague."

## Mercuriale's Theory of Plague

In early modern learned medicine, arguments were separated into three categories: theory (or reason), experience, and written authority. These categories were
intertwined, as theoretical understandings of disease and physiology derived
from interpretations of Aristotle, Hippocrates, Galen, Avicenna, and others.
Similarly, experience included both direct experience—Mercuriale kept records
of the weather during the plague—as well as examples taken from authorita-
tive writings.[63] Experience also included historical accounts, which Mercuriale
referred to as examples (*exempla*). These histories formed a set of particular
instances that could be used to form general conclusions. Accordingly, Mercuriale based much of the theoretical framework and experiential evidence for
plague on his interpretation of ancient writings. The most prominent were the
writings of Galen and the Hippocratic corpus, which contained theories about
disease and cures in addition to accounts of particular epidemics.

His dependence on these sources is particularly evident in his adoption of
the word "constitution" (*constitutio*) to describe the circumstances of epidemic
disease. "Constitution" is a translation of the Greek word *katastasis* (κατάστασις),
which, like the English word, can mean a political organization or the physical
makeup of a particular thing. In the Hippocratic *Epidemics*, *katastasis* is used
in two ways. It is the name for case studies that describe particular examples of
epidemics, and it also refers to the meteorological conditions that were considered to be a cause of epidemic disease, which were called the "constitution of air."
Thus, in the *Epidemics*, the case histories describe the particular "constitution of
air" present during each epidemic. Mercuriale adopted much of the terminology and etiology of the *Epidemics*, which had gained greater scrutiny during the
sixteenth century as a result of the successes of medical humanism, its relevance
for plague, and the growth of medical writings on case histories. Accordingly,
Mercuriale understood the narrative and descriptive account of the plague that
attacked Venice and Padua to be a constitution in the sense of a case history.
Additionally, he understood the air's qualities to have formed a "constitution of
air" that he believed played a significant role in propagating plague.[64]

According to Mercuriale, the constitution of air creates disease by provoking
putrefaction or rotting. Air can foment putrefaction in multiple ways, including
by being corrupt itself. Under this theory, bodies of air possess a temperament,
a mixture of qualities, just as living things, body parts, and medicinal products
do. In Galenic medicine, a temperament can be balanced or possess manifest or

sensible qualities: hot, cold, wet, and dry. While the ideal temperament is balanced, the term is relative. There is no one perfect temperament for everything, but each species has its own ideal one. When the temperament deviates from the ideal, that is, when it becomes imbalanced, the result is what Mercuriale called an intemperance. In people, animals, and their body parts, an intemperance can lead to a predisposition to disease. Intemperances or imbalances of air harm either directly through their excessive qualities or by becoming corrupted and putrid. For this reason, Mercuriale and other physicians considered the southerly wind, called Auster, to be particularly noxious because it brought excessive heat and humidity, creating the ideal conditions for the growth of putrefaction. He noted the wet conditions that coincided with Auster that prevailed in July, September, and October of 1576, when the number of casualties was particularly high in Venice and Padua.[65]

Intemperances in the constitution of air could lead to putrefaction both in air and in bodies. According to this theory, substances, including living bodies, have an internal heat that maintains physical cohesion. For living bodies, this heat was referred to as the innate heat. In humans, the seat of the innate heat is the heart. Following Aristotle and medical theorists, Mercuriale contended that putrefaction takes place when an external heat overcomes and disperses the innate heat, leaving the substance disordered, cold, and without its internal powers.[66] He considered this extreme external heat as preternatural, a term that referred to what does not follow the regular course of nature. This preternatural heat thereby overcomes the heart's innate heat and prevents the body from functioning normally. While Auster could cause putrefaction in the air, impure vapors that arose from the earth—earthquakes were seen as particularly dangerous—or from exhalations produced by marshes, swamps, sewers, waste, and decomposing bodies were also responsible for spreading disease. Following Hippocratic terminology, Mercuriale distinguished older impure fumes from recently putrefied air, or miasmas, which he thought did not substantially corrupt the air.[67]

Mercuriale believed that the heavens, too, could corrupt the constitution of air. This theory, which was promoted by Jean Fernel, proposed that the heavens can transmit imperceptible forms or qualities, which Mercuriale described as secret, hidden, or occult. The air that has assumed these occult qualities attacks the body, leading to putrefaction and the production of poison. Mercuriale, who maintained that God delivers plague and provides mercy from it, described these celestial qualities as divine.

Mercuriale was open to astrological explanations of plague as well.[68] He mentioned eclipses, the supernova of 1572, and a menacing aspect of Mars as portents for the disaster. His discussion of astrology, however, is much more limited than what is found in a number of medieval and early Renaissance plague treatises, which often tied plagues to planetary conjunctions and included detailed discussions of the zodiac.[69] Despite mentioning Mars, Mercuriale did not refer to conjunctions, the zodiac, planetary aspects, or other specialized astrological terms. Furthermore, his discussions of the medieval plague are bereft of astrological considerations, despite the prominence of such explanations during the fourteenth century.[70] Even though astrology was widely used to make predictions about the future during the early modern period, Mercuriale made no reference to it in the section in which he prognosticated about whether the plague would return.

As the most common element among a given population, air was deduced by Mercuriale to be crucial to the spread of epidemic diseases. For the most part, everyone living in a specific place breathes the same air. Since plagues spread throughout the population more quickly and broadly than any other disease, their cause must be equally widespread, making air Mercuriale's chosen culprit. Thus, the crucial factors for determining if the disease in Venice and Padua was "true plague" were not the supposedly infallible signs of buboes but the epidemic's lethal spread, which indicated it originated from the air.

Mercuriale, therefore, defined "true plague" as being widespread within a population and attacking many people at the same time, a majority of whom die. Despite holding that plague is not a fixed disease, he nonetheless saw great similarities among past plagues. He mustered narrations of the plague of Athens during the Peloponnesian War, Hippocrates' description of an epidemic at Cranon in Thessaly in *Epidemics* 2, and histories of the Antonine plague and the Justinianic plague as evidence for aerial causation. Using these accounts, he argued that plague victims have displayed similar symptoms that include fever, nausea, and the appearance of carbuncles. Retro-diagnosis remains difficult, but modern historians believe that some of these earlier plagues arose from different pathogens: while agreeing that the Justinianic plague was bubonic plague, the Antonine plague is now more generally thought to have been smallpox.[71] Mercuriale, however, held that Galen's account of the Antonine plague was directly relevant to the experiences of the sixteenth century. He deemed it impossible that Hippocrates and especially Galen did not write about "true plague."

Nevertheless, Mercuriale conceded that not all plagues were identical. Just as the intemperance and putrefaction of air differ by degree, so do plagues, thereby leading to his classifying plagues based on their severity. The most severe ones, the "greatest plagues," indiscriminately kill all kinds of humans and animals. Death counts are high. Almost all who suffer from the disease die. They often last for years. In this category, he included the plague of the Black Death, the Justinianic plague, the Athenian plague, the Antonine plague, several plagues during the Roman republic, a plague that attacked Constantinople in the eighth century that reportedly killed three hundred thousand, and the Venetian plague of 1528.[72] In several of these plagues, ten thousand people are said to have died daily, with mortality of a third to a half of the population. The plagues detailed by Hippocrates count among "medium plagues," which are less destructive, although Mercuriale cavalierly noted that forty thousand died during a medium plague in the seventh century CE. Lastly, "small plagues" are less destructive, harming only portions of the population and sometimes only specific body parts. A significant portion of those afflicted by the disease survive. This historical analysis suggested to Mercuriale that the outbreak in Venice was not plague before July 1576, because the number of fatalities was low, and that even after it turned into "true plague," it was of medium intensity because less than a third or half of the population had died.

Mercuriale marshalled a vast array of sources as he mined ancient histories and the writings of Byzantine ecclesiastical historians, theologians, and sixteenth-century historians.[73] In addition to the well-known major plagues, he identified epidemics that had occurred throughout the Roman Republic and Empire, in Constantinople in the centuries after the Justinianic plague, and more recently. This employment of history, part of his method of using particulars to build a more universal knowledge, informed his arguments about the causes of plagues, their duration, and their geographical scope. Ancient and medieval historians and theologians provided a counterpoint to medical theorists with respect to contagion. Mercuriale found that Galen and Hippocrates for the most part overlooked this aspect of the subject, despite its frequent appearance in other genres of writing. Ancient historians, ecclesiastical writers, and even the Old Testament sustained the contagious nature of plague or other diseases, suggesting that the concept was widespread in antiquity, even if Galen and Hippocrates minimized or even ignored its role while emphasizing the air's importance in causing epidemics.

Although Mercuriale conceded that ancient authors, including Aristotle, considered contagion, he believed that the origins of a fully developed theory of contagion were modern, first conceived by Girolamo Fracastoro.[74] Fracastoro's fame in part derived from his investigations into the nature of syphilis, a disease that appears to have emerged in Europe in the 1490s during the Italian Wars. Mercuriale and many of his contemporaries called syphilis the French Disease because of the perception that Charles VIII's French troops brought or diffused the disease during the invasion of Italy in 1494. Fracastoro maintained that contagion works on the principle of like to like. That is, contagion can only occur between substances that possess an affinity or a principle of similarity. This idea, which Mercuriale employed, explains why diseases affect only certain species or kinds of people with a predisposition.

Fracastoro held that contagion occurs in three modes: through direct contact, through fomites, and *ad distans* or at a distance. The first mode, direct contact, requires touching a diseased person or substance that transmits the seeds of disease. Fomites refer to intermediary objects that preserve and transmit disease. The term literally means tinder or kindling. In the context of disease, clothing, bedding, and furniture were most commonly identified as fomites, as not all objects were believed to have the capacity to preserve the seeds of disease. Contagion *ad distans* occurs through emanations. Fracastoro gave the example of the eye disorder ophthalmia, which he contended could be transmitted simply by looking at someone with the disease. He presented the example of ophthalmia as being analogous to the supposed powers of the basilisk, a serpent, and the catoblepas, a legendary monster, both of which were believed to kill through sight. In this third category of contagion at a distance, he included plague and pestiferous fevers that he thought were transmitted through the air. For Fracastoro, the three modes of contagion possessed a hierarchy by which diseases that were communicable at a distance were also contagious through fomites and direct contact. Those that were communicable through fomites are also passed through direct contact.[75]

Mercuriale contended that plague was not only contagious but the most contagious disease. Following Fracastoro, Mercuriale believed that the plague spread in three ways and that contagion required similarity between infector and infected, contending that plague was transmitted through the air, through fomites, and through direct contact. He, however, did not refer to contagion occurring *ad distans* but rather held that air acts as a medium for putrid vapors. His explanation of contagion paralleled his understanding of transmission through the constitution of air as he contended that pestiferous vapors emanated from diseased bodies and, at times, were preserved by inanimate bodies like clothes or bedding. These vapors, for Mercuriale, are the vectors of disease. Thus, Mercuriale recognized plague to be contagious, conceiving the nature of contagion to be closely related to the corrupted air that was the primary cause of plague.

## Remedies

Following the dictates of Galenic medicine, Mercuriale held that the cures of plague, just like for any disease, must address the causes of the disease. His remedies, therefore, reflected the multiple layers of the disease's causation: corruption in the air, excessive heat and wetness, occult qualities, putrefaction in the body, and weakness of the heart and its innate heat. Mercuriale divided the remedies into two kinds: those that pertain to individuals and those that concern the state, that is, public health. The remedies for individuals were further divided into three categories: regimen, pharmaceuticals, and surgery. Just as for his understanding of the causes of plague, Mercuriale judged the effectiveness of remedies using the three criteria of authority, reason (or theory), and experience, which included his and his contemporaries' attempts at treating the disease. Given the deadliness of plague, many medieval and early modern remedies for the plague tried to prevent it rather than cure those who were afflicted by it.

Regimen in Renaissance medicine regarded food and drink, the quality of air, sleep and wakefulness, rest and exercise, the elimination and retention of fluids, and a balancing of passions or emotions. Physicians referred to these categories as the six non-naturals, as they were seen to be the external factors of health and diseases as opposed to being part of the body's nature.[76] Generally, Mercuriale's advice about regimen revolved around maintaining a balanced temperament and reducing heat in the body by eating and drinking moderately, eliminating unnecessary movements, purging excessive bodily fluids prone to putrefaction, and regulating the surrounding air.

Given the air's great importance as a cause of the plague, Mercuriale proposed several ways of mitigating its potentially ill effects. He recommended limiting physical exertions of any kind because they increase the quantity of inhaled air. This recommendation fit with his downplaying of contagion through contact, as he contended that quarantines are effective not by eliminating the possibility of contagion but because those who remain closed up move little and consequently breathe less infected air. Even though the amount of inhaled air might be reduced, it cannot be eliminated altogether. Thus, he suggested that air might be qualitatively changed by fumigations, perfumed gloves, washing hands with rose-water and vinegar, and holding balls of aromatics, all of which might help in warding off dangerous vapors. He did not refer to masks; the iconic beaked protective gear did not become widespread until the plague of 1629–1633.[77]

Medications during the Renaissance were for the most part made of botanical and mineral substances that in their unmixed forms were called simples.

Encyclopedic volumes, such as Pier Andrea Mattioli's, based on interpretations of ancient and medieval authors and hands-on experience, catalogued thousands of plants and their properties.[78] Most pharmaceutical preparations required compounding simples. The most famous compounds, theriac and Mithridates' antidote, derived from readings of Galen and other ancient authors.[79] Pharmacists at Venice and elsewhere devoted their energies to perfecting these complex recipes, and city governments regulated their production.[80] Venice, with its commercial empire geared toward trade with the Levant, was a center for the importation and distribution of simples, many of which came from plants native to Asia. The city's large and wealthy urban population fostered the establishment of numerous apothecaries that became focal points for socialization and the exchange of ideas in addition to the sale of medications and cosmetics.[81] By the middle of the sixteenth century, academic physicians in Italy increasingly sought intellectual control over pharmacies and their products, as well as over charlatans who sold tinctures, ointments, and pills.[82] Accordingly, Mercuriale presented specific recipes or prescriptions, which could be brought to a pharmacy or prepared at the patient's home. Later in his career, he wrote a treatise about compounding medicines.[83]

For preventing the plague, Mercuriale recommended medicines that strengthen the heart so that it can ward off preternatural heat and harmful occult forces. Galenic medicine, for the most part, was allopathic and attempted to restore balances by applying qualities that were contrary to those that induced disease. These medications, therefore, should have cooling and drying powers in addition to special properties that repel noxious hidden qualities. Mercuriale also recommended medicines that open up the body's pores and remove fluids that might be liable to putrefaction. He prescribed syrups and broths to be taken orally as well as the application of cautery and the cloaca of a chicken to expel fluids. Cloacae, the sexual orifices of fowl, were widely held to have powers of attraction that could remove harmful matter from the body. For this reason, numerous physicians applied the cloacae of either living or dead chickens to the wounds of those suffering from the plague.[84] The medications that Mercuriale recommended for those suffering from plague and the concomitant pestilential fever correspond closely to those used for prevention. Foremost, they should evacuate and purge the body of putrid and poisonous matter as rapidly as possible.

Medications that purge, however, might not sufficiently remove harmful matter, in Mercuriale's view. For this purpose, he promoted surgical or manual operations. While several authors of plague treatises during these years rejected bloodletting, Mercuriale endorsed the practice, believing that it could purify the body and eliminate plague-inducing fomites.[85] Bloodletting could be accomplished through venesection, cupping, or leeches. Additionally, he recommended vesicatories, which are ointments placed on the skin that provoke blisters and, in theory, eliminate pestiferous matter from the body.

Mercuriale presented additional manual treatments for plague victims who developed buboes or carbuncles. He believed these tumors and welts were caused by the body's attempt to expel harmful matter away from the heart. Consequently, the buboes and carbuncles contain putrid matter that should be removed in order to prevent it from spreading and damaging vital body parts. He recommended cautery, vesicatories, cloaca, unguents, and medicated plasters to open up, clean, and soothe the wound.

Mercuriale thought that governments could take measures to mitigate or reduce the effects of the plague by improving the city's air, separating the sick and their possessions from the healthy portions of the population, and making sure all citizens have adequate food so that they are strong enough to resist the disease. Suggestions for improving the air ranged from the simple—closing windows facing the dangerous southerly winds—to the greatly ambitious—changing the shape of nearby mountains to alter the flow of wind to the city. During the plague, the government should be vigilant in removing the dead and keeping the city's streets clean to prevent foul air from forming. In order to reduce the effects of contagion, Mercuriale urged governments to prevent foreigners from entering and to expel risky segments of the population such as prostitutes and the destitute. The sick should be sent to lazarettos. Wooden structures should be built outside of cities to house those leaving the city, as was done at Padua and Venice. Once the plague has subsided, governments should take care to clean not just the streets but also to purify private homes and incinerate the furnishings of victims of the disease.

## Religion

Medieval and early modern reactions to plague frequently invoked religion. Indeed, in Venice, the government appealed to heavenly intercession, as Venetians from multiple social strata embraced the idea that the plague was divine punishment and could be halted through collective atonement.[86] Mercuriale's treatise reflects a religious understanding of plague; he frequently stated that the ultimate cause of it was God's will. Conversely, hope that a plague will end depends in part on faith in God's mercy. In his view, plague has something divine in it, namely, the occult celestial quality that alters the constitution of air during plagues.

While reflecting common attitudes toward religion and disease, Mercuriale's judgments stand out in respect to some of his colleagues. Many plague treatises referred to God as a cause in merely a perfunctory way before moving on to discussing the physical causes of contagion and the progress of the disease.[87] For example, Mercuriale's contemporary Andrea Gratiolo explicitly separated medical discourse from theology, thereby excusing himself as a physician from speculation about the remote and superior causes.[88] Gratiolo's separation of medicine from theology resonated with large portions of academic culture in northern Italy during the Renaissance. Many professors at Padua and Bologna, for decades if not centuries, had maintained that instruction in philosophy and medicine was distinct from theology in its methods and at times in its conclusions.[89] In an extreme example, during the plague of 1555, Bassiano Lando, a professor of medicine at Padua, wrote that attributing the plague to God's anger was merely a poetic fable.[90] Similarly, physicians who testified in Inquisitorial proceedings in Venice during these years frequently declined to speculate on theology, while willingly offering explanations based on physical and corporeal causes.[91]

Mercuriale's invocations of the divine, therefore, should not be considered merely as reflexive. Rather, they are indicative of his close ties with the Catholic Church, which was at times in opposition to some of his colleagues at Padua and to the Venetian government. Mercuriale formed alliances with Jesuits in Padua and Venice, who were viewed with suspicion by many there. Furthermore, he rebelled against the policy of allowing foreign Protestant students to take degrees, demanding that they attend Mass.[92] Mercuriale personally gained from these associations; and his invocations of the divine, while in contrast with some of his colleagues at Padua, likely endeared him to the papacy that controlled his native Forlì and increasingly exerted its power in the decades after the Council of Trent.

## Plague and COVID-19

In the first part of 2020, many people throughout the world were subject to lockdowns intended to stem the spread of epidemic disease, a new experience for most. Despite the novelty of the situation for many people, numerous infectious diseases have spread throughout the world in the past century. Even after the pandemic of COVID-19 ends, it is more than possible that new ones will arise in the next years. Twenty-first-century societies might regularly face deathly epidemics and constantly live under the threat of them just as late-antique, medieval, and early modern ones did.

In 2020, uncertainty and fear prevailed as the novel coronavirus virus quickly spread and daily death counts rose. Scientists and doctors offered tentative and incomplete answers as they sought to understand the coronavirus's origins, rates of mortality, and modes of transmission. Governments around the world, with varying strictness, imposed public health measures, which were frequently revised. Many who were fortunate enough to own second homes fled major city centers. Workers, small business owners, corporations, industry groups, and financial leaders worried how the health of the economy could be balanced with prohibitions on travel and forced closings of schools, restaurants, gyms, and businesses deemed non-essential. As the closures continued, protest movements arose that objected to the financial and political ramifications of lockdowns. At the onset, because of the novelty of the virus and lack of knowledge of its characteristics, epidemiologists and laypeople alike assessed risk with difficulty whether using statistics based on incomplete data or appealing to experiences of their own, with limited relevance. Many regions that were initially unaffected by the disease failed to act until the disease became rampant. Almost everyone asked how long the pandemic would last, a question for which there is still no clear answer a year after the disease emerged.

During the first months after COVID-19 became a pandemic, many looked to history to find answers. In some cases, this meant to the recent past. Outbreaks of Ebola in the 2010s and SARS CoV-1 at the start of the twenty-first century provided examples of extremely virulent viruses that were contained through vigilant isolation of the infected. Newspapers, magazines, and scientific journals published articles on earlier pandemics, searching for historical perspective into how governments, medical experts, and societies as a whole have reacted to mass disease. The example of the medieval Black Death warned of political extremism and xenophobia.[93] The 1918 influenza pandemic offered a range of lessons about social distancing, early intervention, social trust, and compliance.[94] The Antonine plague that began in 165 CE demonstrated the Roman Empire's resilience.[95] Analyses of influenza pandemics in 1957 and 1968 revealed a subdued public reaction despite widespread death, suggesting to those unhappy with lockdowns that governments were overreacting to COVID-19.[96] Not everyone was so sure that the rush to the past would help. A prominent historian of medicine cautioned about history's capacity to give concrete lessons, since pathogens as well as cultural and social contexts vary greatly from one epidemic to the next.[97]

Indeed, historical analyses reveal diverse cultural, religious, economic, and societal reactions to disease and show that governments' decisions and populations' actions have altered the course of epidemics from the time of Pericles in

the fifth century BCE to the present. The instinct to turn to the past in order
to understand current epidemics is by no means new. Girolamo Mercuriale's
*On Pestilence* tried to answer many of the same questions that have been asked
in 2020. What is the cause of the disease? What role do environmental factors
play? Will it come back? Why are only some people susceptible? What should
the government do? Should there be quarantines? How can individuals protect
themselves? How can the sick be cured? Do institutions, such as hospitals, monasteries, and prisons, pose special dangers to their residents?

Mercuriale turned to history to answer many of these questions. He believed
understanding epidemic disease depended on more than the recognition of
symptoms. The epidemiological profile, that is, the rate of mortality and patterns
of contagion, was key to identifying the disease, and it could only be judged in
relation to epidemics of the past. The results of Mercuriale's turn to history did
not satisfy many of his contemporaries, as he was widely blamed for misdiagnosing the disease in 1576 and for its deadly spread. His historical conclusions
will not likely entirely satisfy today's scientifically minded readers either, given
that Mercuriale, unaware of viruses and bacteria, thought that all epidemics had
the same underlying cause, namely corrupted air. Nevertheless, his reliance on
history to categorize plagues, create epidemiological profiles, and search for the
proper course of action still resonates with today's investigations into past epidemics that look for historical perspective and lessons.

The unfolding of the plague in Venice in 1576 and COVID-19 in 2020
parallel each other in many ways. Mercuriale's example illustrates that political
power and medical expertise have interacted, in different guises, in past epidemics. Indeed, public health and politics are inseparable, since restrictions and
rules invariably reflect the values and priorities of specific groups and pragmatic
decisions do not naturally emerge from medical knowledge. Uncertainties about
the course of disease and about the efficacy of remedies render foresight prob-
lematic. Governments and populations often hesitate to impose or accept highly
restrictive measures until the effects of the disease are dire. Public health actions
can even be seen as experiments, like Venice's attempt to curtail the disease by
blocking movement across the Canal Grande in 1576 or Sweden's decision not to
mandate a lockdown in 2020.[98]

Judgments about who was right or wrong can be hard to establish. It is possible
to condemn Mercuriale for his misdiagnosis of the plague and the lifting of the
quarantine. Yet, it is also possible to sympathize with those he sought to save, who
feared, perhaps rightly, that being sent to quarantine in the lazaretto was in essence
a death sentence. Lifting Venice's quarantine in 1576 might even be considered the

correct decision given the possible vectors of the disease. Was Mercuriale merely a scapegoat for a disaster that would have ensued no matter what he decided? If early modern physicians were unaware of what modern scientists deem to be the cause of the disease, should the quarantines be judged to be merely quaint, ineffective measures—not unlike bloodletting or applying chicken cloaca—that disproportionately weighed on the poor and foreigners? Or might the quarantine have mitigated the disease by reducing the circulation of goods and people and by destroying furnishings, bedding, clothes, and other potential homes to rats and fleas?[99] Even if quarantines and sanitary cordons were ineffective, sixteenth- and seventeenth-century officials in France, Portugal, England, and the Netherlands considered Venice's methods successful and emulated them.[100]

A number of social factors in Mercuriale's time mirror those of 2020. Although the lazaretto was used less as a means to control the poor in Venice than it was in Florence and other Italian cities, nevertheless, social standing greatly determined how one experienced the plague.[101] Residential institutions presented significant risks to their occupants. Wealthy Venetians fled to country estates or stayed in vast palaces, while the city's poor, crowded into small dwellings or shipped to the lazaretto, died in far greater numbers. Many Venetians rebelled against governmental surveillance and restrictions. The rich purchased medicines and fumigants composed of spices and other costly ingredients; the indigent subsisted on substandard and spoiled food. A flood of printed sources shaped public perceptions, describing the horrors of the sickness and speculating about its causes. Almost all these writings, including Mercuriale's, discussed an external source of the disease. They reported that a merchant from Trent, a foreigner in the legal conceptions of early modern Venice, brought the disease to *La Serenissima*.

Historical investigation, along with cutting-edge medical knowledge, guided Mercuriale, just as it does many today. Yet, neither can guarantee success. The past might teach lessons about pandemics, but even what those lessons are is part of historical debate.

## Editions

Despite Mercuriale's reviled role in the plague in Venice, his treatise was a publishing success both in Italy and in northern Europe. It was first published in 1577 in two separate editions, one printed in Padua, the other in Basel. Later editions came out in 1580 in Padua and in 1601 in Venice. Mercuriale's writings on practical medicine were printed frequently in the decades after his death, and *On Pestilence* was included in posthumous collections printed in 1618 and 1623 in Lyon and in 1644 in Venice.[102]

This translation follows the 1577 edition printed at Padua. Several corrections found in the 1601 printing have been incorporated and are indicated in the notes. The Latin text of Girolamo Mercuriale, *De pestilentia* (Padua: Meietti, 1577), is found at https://archive.org/details/depestilentiahie0omerc.

In the notes, all citations of Galen refer to the pagination in *Claudii Galeni Opera omnia*, 20 vols., ed. Karl Gottlob Kühn (Leipzig: Knobloch, 1821–1833). Citations of the Hippocratic corpus refer to the pagination in *Oeuvres complètes d'Hippocrate*, 10 vols., ed. Emile Littré (Paris: Baillière, 1839–1861). Citations of other classical authors follow the abbreviations suggested in the *Oxford Latin Dictionary* and *Liddell-Scott-Jones Greek-English Lexicon*, with a few slight alterations.

# On Pestilence

DE PESTILENTIA

# HIERONYMI

## MERCVRIALIS

### FOROLIVIENSIS

### MEDICI PRAECLARISSIMI

### LECTIONES HABITAE PATAVII

M. D. LXXVII. MENSE IANVARII.

*In quibus de peste in vniuersum, praesertim vero de Veneta, & Pa
tauina, singulari quadam eruditione tractatur.*

A Hieronymo Zaccho, Medico, & Philosopho Patauino,
ex ore ipsius diligenter exceptę, atque in capita diuisę.

NON COMEDETIS
FRVGES MENDACII

**Venetiis , Apud Paulum Meietum Bibliopolam
Patauinum M. D. LXXVII.**

1577

Figure 2. Title page of Girolamo Mercuriale's *On Pestilence* (Padua: Meietti,
1577). Courtesy of Countway Library, Harvard University Libraries.

Lectures held at Padua in January 1577 by Girolamo Mercuriale, the most famous physician from Forlì, on pestilence, in which he discusses with singular erudition plague in general and most of all in Venice and Padua, carefully taken down from his lips and divided into chapters by Girolamo Zacco, a Paduan physician and philosopher.[1]

Venice, Paolo Meietti, 1577

[sig. *2r] [**Dedication**]
Girolamo Zacco sends many greetings to the most illustrious and most excellent Lord Giacomo Boncompagni, Gonfalonier of the Holy Roman Church.[2]

Girolamo Mercuriale, the most famous and greatest physician of our age, held special lectures on pestilence at the university in Padua, which is my homeland, where he teaches medicine, earning the highest praise and admiration of all. In these lectures, he presented so learnedly, clearly, and elegantly the nature of pestilence in general but especially about the one that attacked Venetians and Paduans this year, such that I think nothing more excellent of this kind has been [sig. *2v] written in many years. Since I had taken these from his lips with all the diligence that I could and so many people bothered me every day about them so that I could not satisfy all of them, myself, and Mercuriale himself in any way, I was compelled to have them published. This I did less grudgingly when I saw that the most beautiful occasion had been given to me, most excellent Prince Giacomo, for offering some service to your grandeur, which I had desired most strongly now for a long time. Indeed, your extraordinary virtue is so well known to all as is the singular love for scholars, such that almost everyone points his gaze toward you, like a kind of deity to whom they bring their studies and works. Furthermore, I judged that it would be most pleasing to Mercuriale, whom I know is most dedicated to your grandeur, if these writings of his were published and honored with your name. Additionally, I understand that our city of Padua is much in debt to you, less because you had brightened it with your presence and had presented yourself to delight it, after having left the University of Bologna, than that you honored with singular benevolence Speroni,[3] the jewel of our city, whom all of Italy embraced and admired because of his marvelous integrity, [sig. *3r] rare judgment, and incredible mental force. Then, since I hear that the fear of the plague is not small at Rome—if only this fear was groundless—I thought that I would not act unseemly and futilely if I would send to you, Gonfalonier of the Holy Roman Church, this most beautiful little work, not only for the reason that everyone can be protected from the plague but also because it most carefully discusses the means by which princes of provinces and rulers of cities can avoid its impact on the subjects under their rule. So much the more will everyone grant trust to Mercuriale about this topic, since almost he alone was able to understand truly what helps and what harms, not only from the deep reading of all genres of books but also from an unheard of assiduity in caring for those afflicted by the plague in Padua and Venice and by intimate interaction, so to speak, with them. If this will be pleasing to you, as I hope, we will experience unbelievable joy. Yet, because of your humaneness, you will completely love our most zealous goodwill to you, I think. Farewell.

Padua, Calends of March 1577.[4]

## [1] Proemium

Many things impelled me to discuss the plague at this time. The first was that—since it happened by the mercy of God almighty that these misfortunes were greatly diminished and that we escaped safe from this storm—we seem in a certain sense to give thanks to God himself if we write about this scourge of his. Indeed, the philosopher Themistius said that disputations are pleasing to God that talk about his nature and his effects.[5] The second reason was that, last year, I began to translate the second book of Hippocrates' *Epidemics*, and since it was not allowed to be continued and it was not conceded that it methodically discusses pestilential fever, we will appear to restore this loss if we now again discuss pestilential fever. And the last reason was that, since a certain extreme fear invaded the minds of everybody that it will happen that these afflictions will return again, it will be helpful and welcome to everyone if I will teach most diligently how to avoid this most savage beast. But, since the best method for teaching is that by which universal understanding is obtained by collecting particulars, on that account, I judge it will be opportune if, in order to discuss the plague, [2] I train you about the constitution that occurred. For, it seems to be a most ancient practice and to have been handed down to us by the worthiest Hippocrates.[6]

I will discuss the constitution that took place in six sections. The first will be about everything that generally took place in this calamity. The second section will be about what kind of disease these afflictions should be classified as, whether as true plague or some other kind. The third will be about the cause and origin, since regarding this, it was disputed and is disputed whether it comes from a harshness in the air, or from contagion, or from some other cause. I will examine this matter most carefully, as much as I will be able, and I will discuss contagion so concisely and clearly that perhaps little should be wanting. The fourth will be about why it happened that so many illnesses occurred. The fifth is about what opinion should be accepted: whether it must be feared that this grievous state of misery returns, or whether, instead, we should have hope that at least we, who bow down to God, will remain saved in the future. The last will be about how to treat those struck by the disease if it returns; what princes and republics should do to keep the population healthy; and how private citizens should protect themselves, as much as possible, from imminent danger.

## Index of Chapters

## Chapter 1: On what happened during the plague of Venice and Padua, what bodies suffered, and when the diseases began

For the afflictions, we will look (in order to begin right away) at what occurred and what they were, what kind they were, and when. And the afflictions that developed were either diseases or accidental [symptoms]. The diseases were pestilential, burning, and mild fevers, some of which revealed internal burning and external warmth, or they appeared warm both inside and outside. Additionally, [3] the tumors—mostly small, sometimes larger, at times accompanied by pain, sometimes without—very rarely came to maturation and these were in various body parts, below the groin, and the armpits. Carbuncles, often many, sometimes just one or two, some small, others big, never enormous, were observed in all parts of the body, pustules as well but more rarely.[8] The symptoms that appeared relative to damaged functioning were these: dementia, mental confusion, delirium, stupor, insomnia, severe headache, tinnitus, paralyses, shaking, lack of appetite, nausea, thirst, and a weak, quick, irregular pulse. The symptoms in the alteration of excrement were: drops of blood from the nostrils; vomiting of food, raw humors, bilious humors, worms; raw, fetid, bilious discharges; worms; urine of the ideal color at the beginning, often fiery for some time, a little later thick, disordered, and cloudy. These dispositions appear truly preternatural: reddish color of the face and body; frequent welts on the back; black, purple, and red spots, which sometimes are few, sometimes many, at times narrow, at times wide, sometimes on one or two body parts, sometimes on the entire body, for the most part with a rank odor. Most often death followed these afflictions so that it was sometimes seen that whole families died and, most notably, few survived past the fifth day; most died on or before the fourth day. There was no lack of those who succumbed on the first or second day, which, even if it is told to have happened in other plagues, was nevertheless in no way seen in that most famous one of Athens recorded by Galen, seeing that, as Thucydides narrates, in book 2, and Lucretius, in book 6, the sick in that constitution mostly died on the seventh or eighth day and that the only bodies affected by these afflictions were human bodies.[9] I say this, because, the most ancient writer [4] Homer and Hippocrates, in *On Breaths*, and a nearly countless number of writers recalled plagues in which also animals died, although with the exception of fish, which Aristotle wrote are not affected by plague, in *On the History of Animals* 3.19.[10] Humans, however, were not infected indiscriminately by this disaster, but they were mostly women, and not all women but virgins, girls, and pregnant ones.[11] Among men, boys up to the age of 14 were struck more often than all others, and also some adults, and a few elderly, whom Pliny said were always considered to be minimally affected by plague.[12] And also, the people who suffered this pestilence did not come from all ranks but were commoners, slaves, servants, the incontinent, the dissolute, and those who had absolutely no consideration for life and health.[13]

The start of this affliction took place, as they report, when a certain citizen of Trent, around July, when the plague raged in Trent, landed at Venice, and upon his quick death, the contaminations were spread, and it lasted from that time until the end of December of 1575, such that sometimes one or two persons died and sometimes more. At the beginning of 1576, all the seeds [of the disease] seemed to be completely wiped out. Around the beginning of March, or the end of February, the affliction seemed to recommence, taking advantage of contaminated furnishings, as they report, which, having been closed up, had escaped notice for many months.[14] From that time until July, these seeds produced sometimes more, sometimes less fruit, such that at times many days passed without any death, at times one or two died, sometimes many, sometimes fewer. Around the middle of July, all the illnesses became aggravated, there was a fair number of sick, more frequent deaths, and all of these began to increase during the entirety of August and September and also the beginning of October. If everything is weighed together, it can easily be judged that the disease [5] was at full strength in these months.[15] Afterward, everything began to decline so much that, by the favor of almighty God, almost no traces appear to remain now. This is what happened in Venice. Padua, however, from the beginning of June until the end of May 1576 was free of all pestilential disease, from any hint of it. But, as they say, from infected items brought here, the start and the origin of the slaughter that appeared took place. And at the beginning, everything was mild: few patients and very few deaths appeared; slightly after the middle of July everything worsened; and then, the afflictions increased and took root just like as in Venice to the point that whoever carefully had examined everything could have seen the great similarity and that almost the same constitution of disease was at Padua and Venice. This is what happened in relation to these subjects; for it is not the case that I put forward other topics here that do not pertain to a treatise on medicine.

## Chapter 2: On what kind of disease should these be classified as

Now it must be seen what kind of disease these afflictions should be classified as. It is most established that it comes from the genus of roving diseases, in that it is certain that the same affliction not only raged in our regions but in a great part of Europe. The genus of roving disease was divided into two categories by the ancient physicians, especially by Hippocrates and by Galen, at the beginning of *Epidemics*: one category is called sporadic or dispersed, the other common or most common.[16] Diseases are called dispersed and sporadic whenever diseases of different kinds travel into one or many regions, whether they are non-life-threatening or lethal. Examples of these are ophthalmia, dysentery, various fevers, [6] and other afflictions that the great Hippocrates laid out for us in *Epidemics*.[17] They are called common, whenever diseases of the same kind travel, which are found either in one region or many. If in one region, they are called endemic; some Latin authors called them inhabitant, like Lucretius said, in *On the Nature of Things* 6, the way gout is found in Athens, elephantiasis in Egypt, bronchocele in lower alpine regions, and other diseases in other regions.[18] However, if similar diseases are prevalent not in one region but in many, they are either lethal or salutary. Those that promise a return to health are called by the common name of epidemia or epidemics; we call them simply "popular"; but those common diseases that kill are found to be named pestilences by everyone and are also given the name plague, such that ancient physicians did not leave us any category of plague other than what falls under this class. Indeed, it is clear that these afflictions of ours must be categorized among the common diseases, because there were pestilential fevers and tumors of the same kind, which brought with them the group of reported symptoms. And because, as it was shown, the affliction brought death very frequently—and also this argument can be certain—it must not be categorized as anything other than plague itself. For, Galen said, in *Epidemics* 3.3.19, that plague is not one kind of disease, because a tumor alone, or inflammation alone, or a fever alone must be called plague when many become ill at the same time with a common disease and the majority of the sick die.[19] Therefore, since in this constitution of ours many became ill with one kind of disease and the majority of the sick passed away, it seems most certain to me that it was true plague or we must deny that Hippocrates or Galen ever mentioned true plague.

## [7] Chapter 3: Whether contagion should be included in the definition of plague, and Hippocrates' passage is considered

On this topic, there are two things worthy of examination. The first question is whether, besides the characteristics of plague taken from Hippocrates and Galen, another property must be attributed to plague. For, on the one hand, it seems that also another property is found that follows the nature of plague so that it is a contagious disease. First, in fact quotidian experience shows that those who approach those stricken by plague are readily contaminated. Also, the testimony of Basil the Great, a philosopher and physician, agrees, who in his homely on Psalm 1, recorded that this characteristic is always attributed to plague by physicians and philosophers: that after one person is infected, another is also attacked.[20] The testimony of Thucydides and all historians, who have said the plagues were described as contagious, agrees with this; to be precise, many specified that more died from the contagion than from anything else.[21] On the other hand, there are theories and authorities. The theory is taken from what physicians and philosophers put forward. Let me begin with our leader: Hippocrates, as I have investigated with careful study, nowhere mentioned clearly defined seeds of contagion. And Avicenna, who most carefully attended to the nature of pestilence, did not make any mention of contagion.[22] And, what can seem more wondrous, later [physicians] who followed Galen and Avicenna, both Arab and Greek, seem never to have mentioned contagion. Aristotle, at *Problems* 1.7, said a few rather obscure things.[23] It pleases me that he writes that only plague is extremely contagious, even if he does not mention it at the beginning of *Problems* 7.4, where he discusses other contagious diseases.[24] When he professes to reason why the plague is contagious, [8] he puts forward a feeble enough explanation, writing that plague contaminates those who are closest for no other reason except that the disease is common. Galen also, in *On the Differences of Fevers* 1.2, put forward some brief statements that in no way clearly explain his position on contagion.[25] So, it should be clear that ancient physicians spoke ineffectually and obscurely about contagion. Procopius, in *The Persian War* 2, narrating that greatest pestilence that happened under Justinian in Constantinople, writes that the same plague was certainly most severe but not contagious in any way.[26] Gregory of Nyssa, in an explication of the words of our Savior "What you have done to one of the least of my brothers, you have done to me," elaborated in a long oration in order to show that the pestilence is not contagious; and among other reasons he used this one: that no disease can be contagious just as health is not contagious.[27] Since, he said, there is the same cause for contraries and health and disease are contraries, thus, if any disease should be contagious, also health should be. Because this illustrious writer saw here that experience opposes him, seeing that every day many observe contamination from interaction with those suffering from plague, he said this occurs not because infected people contaminate but because everyone who is seized by plague uses the shared air and has the same internal disposition. Thus, there are so many difficulties from all sides regarding whether this property of contagion must be attributed to plague.

The second question worthy of discussion concerns Hippocrates' words at *On Acute Diseases* 1.9. In this passage, it seems that he thinks some sporadic diseases are harmful, indeed even more lethal than pestilences.[28] This opinion is contrary to the view shared by all physicians, especially Galen at the beginning of *Epidemics,* where also he, just like all others, makes pestiferous diseases more lethal than all others.[29]

For the answer to the first question, I say it must be unequivocally established that plague is contagious, no matter what, [9] and even maximally contagious. Consequently, it seems that contagion must be necessarily prominent in its definition or description, like a certain property that is always part of it, and even to it alone, seeing that, as Aristotle says in the cited passage of the *Problems*, only plague, of all diseases, is maximally contagious;[30] even if leprosy and phthisis have whatever it is that makes them contagious diseases, they are not maximally contagious so that contagion is continually one of their effects. But I hope in this treatise that I will say much that is worth knowing about the nature of contagion and about all of its characteristics.

But what should we say about the authorities that have been presented? There is no lack of most erudite men, who said, seeing that the ancients disregarded contagion, it is as if they had buried this famous topic. But it seems truly difficult to me to excuse the ancients, who pursued other topics of little importance with lengthy speeches but disregarded this extremely difficult topic full of the greatest uncertainties. Therefore, I am of the opinion, that contagion was in no way unknown to the physicians of old, because there were ancient writers, the Greek historians, who spoke of the contagion in plagues. But they passed over it in silence, in my view, because they did not recognize any kind of contagion except that which occurs through air, as you will see later on, and for this reason they described it under the category of air. Otherwise, you prefer to say they disregarded contagion, since they did not think it was a cause of the formation of pestiferous diseases. As for Galen, in the cited passage of *On the Differences of Fevers*, look, I beg, at how he wavers about contagion. He says, in book 1, that it is not safe to interact with those affected by plague and then that there is a danger of dying for those who interact with them; after this, he says little or nothing at all about contagion.[31] Would have Galen, who (I say with all due respect) is usually extremely verbose even about matters of little importance, as everyone knows, passed over contagion in silence, if he had thought it has a role in the cause of plague? I shall never be led to believe this unless better arguments convince. [10] What should we say about Procopius? I have his text in Greek manuscript, in which those phrases are missing, which are in the Latin codex in which he reports that the plague itself was not contagious. Gregory of Nyssa, although he was an illustrious philosopher, was not an expert in medicine, yet he gave a sermon about it in that passage.[32] Having set forth this example of plague and diseases, it was satisfactory for him to proceed to his larger purpose and aim. As for why health is not contagious but only disease, Aristotle explains it to us in *Problems* 7.4.[33]

In order to answer the second question, it should be stated briefly: among disease nothing more lethal is found than pestilential disease. In fact, Hippocrates' opinion, in *On Acute Diseases* 1, in my view, must be interpreted such that sporadic diseases, if they are acute, are more lethal than all other diseases, except pestiferous ones.[34]

## Chapter 4: Plague is defined, and it is shown
## that it was true plague in Venice and Padua

And so let us establish this definition or description of plague in this way: namely, that it is a common disease, infecting many different regions at the same time, that is lethal and maximally contagious; it is called a disease without qualification, just as I said in yesterday's lecture based on Galen's view in *Epidemics* 3.3.[35] Plague is not one fixed disease; but any disease can be plague if it strikes many at the same time and kills a majority of them. It is called a common disease, in opposition to sporadic ones. It is said to infect many different regions, in opposition to endemic diseases, which always harm just one region. It is called lethal, in opposition to those common diseases, which are simply called epidemics, [11] which Hippocrates discussed in most of the *Epidemics*. It is called maximally contagious to the extreme, not only in opposition to pestilential fevers—which are not contagious and which occur without plague, and it is satisfactorily established that very many arise without any contagion—but also because, as I said just before, its nature is best illustrated through this property. For, although diseases other than plague are contagious, it [contagion] is proper to plague—which the ancient physicians treat clearly as a common disease—since, still, there is no plague without contagion and it is the most contagious among all contagious diseases "above all," as Aristotle says, whose use of the word *malista* Gaza does not translate appropriately enough.[36] It seems this word must be added necessarily in order that the description embraces its entire nature as much as possible. And you should not marvel that I said pestilential fevers occur without plague because Galen said this most clearly and most plainly, in *Epidemics* 3.57 and also in *On Prognosis from Pulses* 3.4, where he writes most clearly that pestilential fevers arise without plague.[37]

Since the definition and nature of plague is now established in this way, let us see if this entire definition of plague fits with this constitution of ours. For, if it will fit, we will be certain this was the true plague. First, it was most clearly a disease; steady burning fevers, tumors, and carbuncles are diseases, which, as I said in the historical account, appeared most frequently. Who would doubt it was also a common disease? Since a large part of Europe was attacked by this misfortune at one and the same time. Furthermore, it is most clear that many different regions became ill simultaneously: for, Austria, Transylvania, and other Germanic nations and many other populations suffered from the plague at the same time and in the same way as in Italy, Cividale del Friuli, Venice, Padua, Milan, Calabria, Sicily, and Illyria. In the same way, also through our great suffering, we learned by experience that these diseases [12] were lethal and max-imally lethal, since most of the sick died. There is a great deal of most excel-lent testimony that this plague was contagious, which I will not recount to you, since everybody has his own examples. If, therefore, all the characteristics of true plague, either handed down by the ancients or laid down and added by us, are found in this constitution of ours, we should not hesitate to assert that it was the true and genuine plague, although it was not such in that time when more or less three people died each day, since, as is most clear, the most important char-acteristic that is required according to Galen was missing, namely, that simulta-neously many become sick and many perish. And let no one say that greater or lesser intensity changes the species and, therefore, it must be identified as plague anyway, when few rather than many died. Since, if, as no one denies, plague is a common disease, in what way, I ask, will we call it a common disease unless many people fall ill? As we taught according to Galen, how can we call what has the same kind of ailments plague, unless the majority of the sick die; indeed in other times there were occasionally acute diseases and pestilential fevers which quickly slaughtered the sick, but no one called it plague because it was not a common disease, that is, it did not afflict many.

## Chapter 5: On the causes of plague

Now it remains that we discover the causes of this plague. We will discover this, if we will examine the causes of true plague. Some of the causes of true plague are internal, others external. The internal causes are a preternatural, putrid heat and a poisonous, putrefying humor. I say a preternatural heat because, even if it often happens in cases of plague that neither internal nor external altered heat [13] appears perceptible, nevertheless it can never happen that this is a natural heat, in that nearly all operations of natural heat—concoction, attraction, and all other functions, which derive from the agency of innate heat—fail immediately. The putrid and poisonous matter, which is the internal cause of plague, however, is not made up of one type, but nearly all humors are mixed together, are thrown into disorder, and putrefy; and this putrefaction is not slight but very significant, as Hippocrates rightly had said it was decay, using the common word, which also Galen most straightforwardly said often, having imitated Hippocrates.[38] But not only is the putrefaction significant in this matter, but there is something else that is more remarkable, which produces those effects in plague that putre-faction never appears to make. I find that among earlier writers on medicine it was disputed what this remarkable quality is. There was no lack of those who thought it was nothing other than some hidden and unmanifest quality, among whom the top place is held by the most diligent and intelligent Fernel, who in *On the Hidden Causes of Things* laid out most carefully this opinion.[39] However, Altomare disputed against Fernel, showing that, in no way, was any unmanifest quality present but simply a certain extreme degree of putrefaction occurs, which is responsible for everything.[40] But since it is widely recognized that not all pestiferous fevers have the same putrefaction—indeed it often happens that quicker deaths and more severe symptoms arise when lesser signs of putrefaction appear—it seems necessary to me to assert that besides the putridness some occult, poisonous power is present in this matter, which all physicians and especially Galen write is present in medication and harmful poisons.[41]

For the external causes of plague, I thereby state, that two causes perpetually conspire to produce the plague: without doubt, the air itself and contagion. [14] Hippocrates seems to me to have shown with the clearest demonstration that air contributes to producing plague, which Galen and Avicenna appear to follow.[42] It is this: plague is the most common disease; therefore, it comes from the most common cause; the most common cause is air; therefore, plague necessarily comes from the air. This argument of Hippocrates' was so convincing among the writers of medicine that it is almost impossible to find anyone who does not think true plague arises from the air. Thus, after God, air is the cause of true plague. I say after God, seeing that, as Galen mentions, the ancients closely ascribe the causes of pestilence to God, which also Avicenna (*Metaphysics* 10.1) and Avenzoar do not censure in any way.[43]

But a question arises about why Hippocrates said that only air is the cause of pestilence, when Galen, in the book *On Good and Bad Foods and Juices* and in *On the Differences of Fevers* 1.3, shows that pestiferous diseases also arise from poor diet.[44] In order to remove this difficulty, Altomare said that what Galen describes as being generated by an improper diet were indeed diseases, but in no way were they the plague but rather simply pestiferous diseases.[45] But this response of Altomare does not untie the knot completely, for, Galen, in his commentary on *On the Nature of Man* 2.4, said that Hippocrates said correctly that a common disease comes from a common cause, but did not say correctly that it comes only from air, given that also an improper diet and vapors emanating from putrid water and caves can produce common diseases, the same thing that Hippocrates himself left in writing about the constitution in Ainos.[46] Therefore, as we approve Hippocrates' view, I think it is sufficient to say that it can be understood to be air alone or together with other causes. If we understand it to be air alone, clearly air alone is not always the cause of common disease or pestilence; but, if we understand it together with other causes, air is always a cause of common disease. Or, [15] we can also say that common disease is of two kinds, some common to one region, others common to many regions. Diseases common within one region, which are called endemic by the Greeks, come to be from an improper diet, from vapors that rise from water and the earth. The rest, which are common within many regions, always originate from the air, wherefore it is established clearly by Hippocrates and all writers that true pestilence always arises from the air.

## Chapter 6: The Venetian and Paduan plague originated from the air

Therefore, we can start this description of our plague. Every plague comes from the air, as has been proved. Our plague, as we described in depth, had all the characteristics of true pestilence; therefore, our plague was formed from the air. When I say our plague, I mean all those diseases that laid waste to these regions. But, because plague has additionally something unknowable of the divine, it should be useful to add, besides the demonstration reported based on the authority of physicians, other signs recorded by historians and others with which we can confirm at least in a probable manner that this plague originated from the air. The signs of this sort have all been learned through observation. And, as I have been able to learn, there are two kinds: some are antecedent, others are accompanying. The antecedent signs are previous earthquakes, comets or unusual stars, aerial fires, eclipses, leap year, monsters, animals generated out of putrid matter, and plagues that are roving elsewhere. I shall also add two others to these signs, taken from Philostratus, in book 4 and 8 of *The Life of Apollonius* and also in the book *On Famous Men* (who went to Troy). This writer reports that Apollonius of [16] Tyana, a very great man, predicted the plague of Ephesus because he, who had the most ideal temperament, had suffered from disease. This philosopher nearly prophesized it was necessary that others would become ill because of a defect of the air, since he did nothing wrong and yet became ill. Additionally, he reports that wolves inflicting damage to humans usually foretell the plague in humans.[47] If we consider all these signs and compare the past situation of our regions at least many of these signs, if not all, were present beforehand. There were earthquakes in Padua and

Venice but especially in Ferrara.[48] But this tells us nothing, since Ferrara was not touched by the plague, as exhalations emitted from an earthquake can be spread far and wide and not touch the closest regions. Additionally, we had an unusual star in the previous years, about which in Germany it was disputed whether it was a comet, and there are writings about it.[49] During the entire year that insolent star Mars was visible, which instilled in many wonder and stupor and a kind of terror in a great number of people, who recount that they had seen it darken at times. We had a leap year. In the past year, if you remember, an incredible quantity of caterpillars was seen in the streets and on walls and windows, which are animals that originate from putrefaction.[50] We had that monster at Venice.[51] It is clear that there were roving plagues, like we had in Constantinople, Sicily, and Trent. That year we had an eclipse.[52] So, if we like to do what the ancients did, we can clearly say that the usual signs preceded our plague from the air. I will not pass over that it was told to me that wolves in that year attacked a great number of farms in the Paduan countryside.

The accompanying signs are those symptoms, those diseases, which always accompany every plague that comes from the air. These are burning fevers, mild fevers, headaches, deliria, carbuncles, tumors, sudden deaths, and annihilations of families. [17] All these incidents happened in them and also in ours, if it will please you to look at all plagues that come from the air. In fact, if you compare the plague narrated by Ovid, in *Metamorphoses* 7, the one described by Hippocrates, in *Epidemics* 2 about Cranon, the one described by Thucydides, in *The History of the Peloponnesian War* 2, and by Lucretius, in *On the Nature of Things* 6, those that Galen reports happened during his time, and the extremely great plague that Evagrius, in *Ecclesiastical History* 4, and Nicephorus, [in *Ecclesiastical History*] (17.18), write about, if it was the same most horrible plague that occurred under the Emperor Justinian at Constantinople that Procopius describes, in *The Persian War* 2, if, I say, you compare these and countless others to our plague, you will see the greatest similarity, if I should not say identicalness.[53]

Other signs cannot be scorned in addition to these, but the most valuable is that, in the whole time during which the plague lasted, especially in cities, it was rare to see those who were attacked by any other kind of disease, which all these physicians take for a most certain argument that plague comes from the air. Indeed, those who were attacked at the beginning by a tertian [fever] or some other disease, their diseases were mostly (all of which Thucydides also noticed to be especially distinguishing characteristics of the plague) transformed into them.[54] The most erudite physicians of this city report to you that there were those who were wounded and their wounds were transformed into plague.

Something else significant pertains to confirming a defect of the air, which I myself observed in these regions and I heard happened in others equally affected by plague, namely that a majority of those who died without any suspicion of plague, after their death, had their backs befouled by welts and wide spots, which we are accustomed to see very rarely in other times. Moreover, there were countless ones, who, aware that they had handled nothing that was infected, nevertheless were carried off by this disaster. Additionally, if you choose to ask, you will hear about countless people whose groins and armpits [18] swelled up with pains and that various tumors erupted spontaneously without any noteworthy damage. Indeed, since these afflictions were not pestiferous and they were seen much less often or never in past years, it is certainly necessary to acknowledge that the cause was the present year's constitution and some defect of the air, under which bodies predisposed in different ways became ill, sometimes mildly, sometimes dangerously. But perhaps it is not wrong to add another reason: that in July, when the disease worsened in Venice and Padua, also rains began, which were slight, gentle, and nearly continuous, such as those that Hippocrates reported in Cranon, and it is clear that the constitution endured a southerly wind for almost all of September and October.[55] We also had another calamity that shows the air was infected: the sparseness of all harvests from the earth, which although they were abundant nevertheless lost their usual robustness. Also, it should not be disregarded that everyone observed that in this year no or very few cicadas sang. Cicadas, as you know, feed on dew, and it seems reasonable that they were exterminated or silenced, having been deprived of their customary nourishment.[56] Also, there is no lack of those who openly admit that they observed that very rare birds were seen when the pestilence raged in these regions. Therefore, we hold from the reported description and from additional signs that our pestilence originated from the air.

## Chapter 7: What was the defect in the air; and how the air is said to have become defective and induced the plague

Now, let us see what this defect in the air was. I declare it was some kind of quality harmful to human life, capable of producing pestilential diseases in ready and predisposed bodies. Fernel, a most erudite [19] and intelligent man, in *On the Hidden Causes of Things* 2, arrived at the opinion that there is a secret and occult quality of such a kind.[57] Altomare, however, who, like all other learned men, thought that all true plagues arise from the air, tried, against Fernel, to demonstrate with many arguments that there was no secret quality in pestilential air but only a manifest one, that is, one arising from putrefaction.[58] Truly, I am of the opinion that plague can arise both from a manifest quality of the air itself and also from a concealed quality. Hence, I contend it can arise from a concealed quality, since if in the air a celestial and occult generative quality comes to be, as Aristotle often showed in *On the Generation of Animals* 2 and elsewhere, then it must be admitted that sometimes also secret corrupting qualities come to be in the air.[59] That during many plagues assistance was received from concealed and secret antidotes also supports this. For, Galen writes that plague is sometimes cured by Armenian bole, sometimes by human urine, sometimes by theriac.[60] Therefore, if the concealed remedies brought comfort, it stands to reason that there was also something concealed that harmed. This occult quality or unmanifest defect can be induced in the air by two causes, the first is from the stars. It is not through their nature that the stars make something evil through their essence but accidently. And not only astrologers but also the great Avicenna confirmed that this happens. Indeed, truly also Hippocrates or Polybus seems to have perceived this, who, in *On Diseases* 4, while establishing three principles of diseases, writes that one of these is that whatever comes from the heavens is unsuitable and contrary to regimen, should it occur.[61] The second is that this secret quality can be induced into the air from deformed vapors that rise from putrefied waters or caves. For, Galen said, in his commentary on *On the Nature of Man* 2.5, that vapors that rise from these kinds of putrefied things never harm through a manifest quality but by a property [20] of the substance.[62] Two examples from histories magnificently bear witness that the most severe plagues can originate from these kinds of exhalations and vapors. The first is the history in which it is narrated that once in Babylonia in the temple of Apollo a golden arc of wondrous age breathed out a most dangerous exhalation and thence a plague spread, which raged most gravely all the way to the Parthians.[63] The second is in Ammianus Marcellinus, who writes that during the era of Emperor Marcus Verus, after a temple was sacked and an effigy of Apollo was brought to Rome, soldiers of Avidius Cassius found a narrow perforation, from which, once opened, a most dangerous spirit exhaled out, which brought about the worst plague.[64] Moreover, there is that manifest quality that is generated in the air from the corruption of its substance that sometimes becomes so strong that it causes the plague but sometimes is less strong so that it causes only common diseases and epidemics.

Here we must carefully observe four matters. One is that air can be understood in two ways, either as the simple element or as a body composed of the element and vapors or those corpuscles that Democritus and Epicurus discuss. If we take air in the first way, in no way can its substance be corrupted and Aristotle's view in *On the Length and Shortness of Life* and *Problems* 25.20 should be interpreted in this way.[65] In these passages, the leader of philosophers said that air does not become corrupted or putrefy. But if we understand air to be a mixed body, then there is no doubt that air putrefies and is corrupted with respect to its substance, since Aristotle understood this very thing at the beginning of *Meteorology* 4.[66] But know this: when air is corrupted in this way, it is corrupted because of old vapors mixed into it; I say old because those vapors recently putrefied that are mixed in with air and which are called *miasmata* by Hippocrates in his language or miasmas by us are another kind of corruption that must not be called substantial corruption in a proper sense.[67] [21]

The second thing that must be noted is: when we say air is putrefied substantially, in no way must this be understood as the air becoming poisoned, but we understand that thanks to this corruption it becomes suitable for generating poison in all predisposed bodies. The reason why air cannot become poisoned seems to be that, as Aristotle said as well at *Problems* 25.20, air is replete of much fire; fire, however, as you know, pushes poison as well as other things far away.[68] Another reason is the deliberation of nature, wise and most learned in all things, as Hippocrates said, which, since it strives to preserve the nature of animals, is always accustomed to make provision so that poisons are produced in small quantities. But if air should become poisoned, the amount of poison would be most abundant; and since air is breathed continually by all animals, if just a little bit of air should become poisoned such that it is a poison, it would immediately kill all living creatures, just as we see that any kind of poison kills every kind of animal, especially humans; and it would kill far more than all other poisons, because other poisons are consumed just once and in a small quantity, but air is great in quantity and pulled into the body continually.

The third thing that must be noted is that pestiferous air leads to the generation of poison in our bodies, since it induces a kind of preternatural heat harmful to the natural [heat] in predisposed bodies, which, when it mixes with and breaks down the innate heat, then it follows that all the humors of our body, deprived of the protection of innate heat, are straight away mixed together, putrefy, and consequently take in the poison's nature.

The fourth is: that the fixed quality in the air is called manifest by me, in that, even if there occurs a mutation and alteration of the substance of air, nevertheless, this alteration and this mutation is caused by some manifest intemperance of the air, which is called a manifest intemperance by Hippocrates wherever

[22] a *katastasis* or "constitution" is found.[69] This intemperance, just as it can
vary and differ, causes different kinds of common diseases. For, if it is hot and
wet, it will be such that it corrupts the air's substance or such that it only alters
it. If it corrupts the air's substance—I refer not to the elementary substance but
the mixed one—it leads to plague, just as Galen most lucidly taught at *On Temperaments* 1.4, where he writes, if this hot and wet intemperance remains for the
whole year a great pestilence develops; but if it remains only for part of the year, a
smaller pestilence develops.[70] However, an intemperance of this sort can come to
be in the air from celestial forms, as Avicenna, at [*Canon*] 4.1, teaches; it can also
come to be from exhalations and winds.[71] If this intemperance, however, alters
the substance of the air, simple epidemic diseases, not pestilential ones, arise, as
there are various kinds of catarrhs; the other intemperances of air (hot and dry,
simply hot, cold and wet, and cold and dry) never lead to plague but only to
epidemic disease, the most famous examples of which you have in Hippocrates
at *Epidemics* 1 and 2 and in other books.

## Chapter 8: What Hippocrates calls divine in diseases: whether other constitutions of air besides hot and wet can give birth to plague

But before we go forward, two topics worthy of questioning rise up. The first is
what did the divine Hippocrates want to convey to us in *Prognostics* 1, when he
writes that a physician, wishing to give a prognosis for diseases, must pay attention to what is divine in diseases.[72] The second is whether it is true that constitutions of air other than hot and wet never give birth to plague.

[23] As for the first topic, Galen, after having explored others' views, seems
to have established that according to Hippocrates there is nothing divine in diseases besides the intemperances of air— the constitutions of air. But I use the
same argument against Galen that he uses in this commentary against others:
that certainly it cannot be easily found that Hippocrates in other places used
this word "divine" for the constitution of air. For, at the start of *On the Nature of
Women*, whoever is that author commonly placed under the name Hippocrates
by the crowd, writing that the cause of disease in humans is *to theion*, that is, "the
divine" and therefore must originate *apo tōn theiōn* [from divine things], surely
does not mean the constitution of air.[73] Therefore, in the interpretation of this
passage, the opinion of Stephanus of Athens and Taddeo the Florentine seems

more convincing, who said that what is called divine by Hippocrates, is indeed what is in the air yet caused by the heavens, just as he also established the celestial cause of diseases in *On Diseases* 4.[74] For, as I also taught to you before, it cannot be doubted, according to the views of all physicians, that just as the heavens imprint hidden qualities on these terrestrial bodies, they also imprint on the air itself a secret quality of this kind, either harmful or benign, just as most famously Avicenna taught, in [*Canon*] 4.1 and 1.3.5.1, where he discusses pestilence.[75] Thus, Hippocrates called not any constitution of air "the divine" in diseases but the secret constitution and quality. Hippocrates spoke in a similar manner in the book that is mistitled *Peri sarchōn,* or *On Fleshes,* and should rather be titled *Peri archōn,* that is, *On Principles.* For, he said there that our heat is something immortal that understands all things.[76] And I do not think he meant anything different at *Epidemics* 2.1, when he wrote that disease and season correspond with each other, unless something is altered in a higher nature.[77] Thus, also [24] the divine Plato, an imitator of Hippocrates, [wrote] in *Epinomis* that there is something divine in all reproduction, which Aristotle suggested similarly to us at the beginning of *On the Generation of Animals* 2.[78] Incidentally, I think Homer wanted to say the same thing to us when he writes that Apollo sends pestilence to men using arrows.[79]

As for the second proposed question, what makes it difficult is that Galen, at *On Temperaments* 1.4, explicitly sustained that only a hot and wet constitution gives birth to pestiferous diseases.[80] On the other side, Ammianus Marcellinus, in book 19, writes that philosophers and famous physicians taught that pestilences are generated from excessive cold, heat, wetness, or dryness.[81] Furthermore, there are histories that ought to have a place in our most weighty arguments. The prince of the Latin poets, in *Aeneid* 3, writes that in Crete a plague occurred because of a hot and dry intemperance.[82] Livy, at 1.4, narrates that at Rome a plague occurred as the result of a great drought, which is also found to have happened some other time in the writings of Nicephorus Callistus, [at *Ecclesiastical History*] (15.10), when he writes that from a drought a plague arose, in which people with inflamed eyes first lost sight and then, having progressed to coughing, perished; he adds that for this plague no remedy was found.[83] Avenzoar, also, a very great physician, as you know, taught that plagues come to be from dryness.[84] There is no lack of those who teach that it also comes from a cold intemperance, and they say that a plague of this sort occurred in AD 1119.[85] For the solution to this controversy, it ought to be established among you that in no way can true plague come from any intemperance other than wet and hot. This is also what the great Aristotle seems to have suggested at *Problems* 1.21, where he writes that a pestilential year came about once when the sun's heat carried many vapors from the earth and a wet constitution was formed.[86] But what will we say [25] about the examples of historians? It is nothing other than that these plagues were not made only from the reported intemperances but also from other causes; for, with these intemperances there was always a lack of grain, or wars, or earthquakes, or some other cause that, together with these intemperances, could have caused the plague, namely, by spoiling the air.

## Chapter 9: Which qualities of the air were the cause of plague in this period

But since we have already established these answers, now it is fitting that we determine what quality was in the air in this period that gave occasion to the generation of plague. I think there were three things in the air in this period. The first were evil and foul vapors that, as I said, infected the air with respect to its whole substance. I am led to think this because the places that were first attacked by plague in Italy are exposed to impure exhalations. For, this is true for Messina in Sicily; Trent is just as if it was positioned in a kind of cavern, circled by mountains on all sides. Clearly no one doubts that Mantua is subject to impure exhalations. But what city is more infested by impure exhalations than the city of Venice? Even our Padua, because of its proximity, probably could have had air contaminated by impure exhalations.

The reason why in this year more than in others impure and pestiferous exhalations rose must be related to the influence of the heavens, whether we should prefer to say hidden influences or motion and light.[87] There is no doubt that heaven's instruments do not always act in the same way but sometimes more sometimes less, just like how the sun with its own light lifts these exhalations sometimes more sometimes less, as is gathered from Aristotle himself at *Problems* 1.21.[88] The other quality that was in the air in this [26] year was manifest from the intemperance of the air itself. For, if you recall accurately, last year winter was mild enough, snow was rarely seen; in the previous summer it rained often; in the following spring the heat started quickly, then it abated, and we had most frequent rains for the entire summer; the fall was characterized by Auster, hot and humid, so that, since the proper temperament was not preserved in any season of the year, it is no wonder if pestiferous winds arose, seeing that, as Hippocrates said, in *Aphorisms* 3, when the seasons do not preserve the proper constitutions, irregular diseases arise.[89] And it is not true that there was already plague before the rains and constitution of Auster, since, as I said and as I will say, there was no true plague in these regions before July 1576 but only pernicious and pestilential fevers. The last quality that was in the air was some kind of occult property from the heavens impressed onto the air. Because of it, it happened that some conditions appeared in roving diseases to which almost no natural explanation can be assigned, just as also usually appears in every plague, so that, as Galen correctly said, the ancients always looked to the Gods for remedies in a pestiferous constitution.

## Chapter 10: What disposition of the body is necessarily required for being susceptible to plague, and what kind it is

But in order that we arrive perfectly at the truth of this solution, you must understand two things about this topic. The first is that no quality can be found in the air that is strong enough that it can cause plague or another disease unless the disposition of the bodies is appropriate, which is a view believed not only by philosophers but also by all physicians, just as Hippocrates, in *On Breaths*, and Galen, in *On the Differences of Fevers*, clearly teach.[90] The disposition of bodies susceptible to the plague and the reception of impressions from the air is twofold, hidden and manifest, just as the active quality of the air is also twofold, hidden and manifest, although Fernel, a most intelligent man in other respects, held that only a secret quality is in all pestilences.[91] The body's occult predisposition to the plague is nothing other than a certain property of the heart, which by no means repels all harmful impressions from it. I think that Avicenna wanted to indicate this property to us when he spoke about the property of the disposition, in [*Canon*] 4.1 on the chapter on plague.[92]

I am persuaded by two arguments to believe that there is an occult property of the heart of this kind. The first is because, just as you know from Galen, in *On the Differences of Fevers* 1, the air that will generate the plague attacks the heart itself first and in no way will the plague arise before the heart's condition is assaulted.[93] I say that it assaults the condition of the heart, in that the spirits and humors and then also the solid structure itself are mixed with pestiferous air.

The second argument is: how will we be able to assign the true explanation for many events unless we stipulate that there is this occult property for the heart? For, you will see during the plague that many who are constantly in the company of the infected patients, who have bodies completely full of impure humors, are never attacked by the plague even when they live immoderately and do everything that should lead to death, just as Evagrius tells happened in that great plague and just as happened also in ours, in which very many undertakers and countless others, who most frequently dealt with the sick and infected things, survived.[94] Conversely, you will see many with a completely healthy body with the best temperament, living extremely prudently, who nevertheless at some very slight opening are affected by plague. This occurrence can be explained by no other reason [28] except that those who are not attacked by plague have some kind of property in the heart by which they repel all pernicious impressions from themselves but those who easily succumb to plague have a hidden inclination in the heart, by which it happens that the heart cannot resist impressions and readily receives all of them. The manifest disposition in humans can be many sided: it can come from the temperament and from the build of the body, from the sex, from the body's temperament, because hot and wet bodies, bodies full of impure humors, and loose and rarefied bodies, as Avicenna said, are extremely prone to succumbing to plague.[95] And this is the reason why women are frequently attacked by the plague, since they have bodies full of impure humors. And among women, especially pregnant ones are most vulnerable to plague because of the retention of menses and because, as they have a fetus in the uterus, their bodies are hot and wet, and because of the heat, they breath in a lot of air. And similarly, virgins who are of marriageable age are extremely [vulnerable]. And Jacques Despars, a most weighty author, in the commentaries on [*Canon*] 4.1, said that he had proved through experiment that the poison generated in virgins during the plague has no cure.[96] And we observed this in our outbreak, namely, all virgins of marriageable age who became ill perished. The cause of this is in part the sensual desire by which virgins become nearly wild; in part the retention of seed and the flowing of menses; and in part their gluttony, on account of which they sate themselves with impure foods and fruits. Boys are equally extremely vulnerable to plague, partly because of their disordered way of life; partly because of their heat and wetness; and because, as Rhazes said in *For Almansor* 5, they draw in a lot of air and therefore are very full of its defect.[97] Thus, those who exercise the body, since they are forced to breath quickly, are also simultaneously attacked by the plague. Therefore, slaves are readily brought down by this kind of affliction. There is one more thing besides [29] these that greatly predisposes human bodies susceptible to plague: fear, as bodies rendered weak by it succumb to the plague more quickly. These are what most render bodies prone to susceptibility to the plague.

## Chapter 11: The air's quality is at times stronger, weaker, and neutral, and what it was in Venice and Padua

The second matter that we have determined to be worthy of consideration is that the air's quality, both secret and manifest, is not always disposed in one and the same way. For, sometimes the injurious quality of this kind is very intense such that even bodies only moderately predisposed are poisoned and infected; sometimes it is so weak that it needs a great suitableness in the body; and sometimes its condition is in the middle, such that it is neither so weak nor so intense.

When this quality of the air is very intense, it gives birth to extraordinary and the greatest pestilences. These extraordinary pestilences are those in which also animals are slaughtered and most men die. That plague that is recounted by Ovid in *Metamorphoses* 7 was this kind.[98] The one at Athens, recounted by Thucydides and by Lucretius, was also this kind, about which they said almost no man was found at that time whom neither disease, nor death, nor grief touched.[99] The plague at Rome during the time when Camillus the Great died was this kind.[100] The one under the emperors Vespasian and Commodus was also this kind, as Eusebius recorded for posterity in the *Chronicles*, in that 10,000 people died every day in Rome, but in this one there were 2,000.[101] The plague that Procopius narrates, in *On the Persian War* 2, was also this kind, when in the city of Constantinople often, on any given day, 10,000 people died.[102] Also, it is also told that under Leo the Isaurian in Constantinople [30] 300,000 people died from the plague.[103] The many plagues recounted by Galen were also this kind and especially that one, by whose violence, nearly all of Europe was depopulated. Platina narrates that more died than survived under Pope Benedict VIII.[104] Jacques Despars writes that in that plague that began in 1345 almost half of all humankind of the whole earth was wiped out.[105] This plague lasted five years and because of it many towns were cruelly destroyed; and the city of Venice, as Sabellico narrates, was forced to summon foreigners and bestow them with citizenship because of the extraordinary destruction of the population.[106] There was also a great pestilence in 1528, when a third of the population died, as many of the most famous writers say. Thus, these great and extraordinary plagues were the result of an intense harmful quality of the air.

However, the quality in the air is weak whenever the destruction lasts for a short period of time and few people die, and not all kinds of people. There was this kind of plague, as Livy narrates in 4.1, during the consul of Quintus Fabius Augustus and Gaius Furius Pacilus, when more became ill than died.[107] I think that also those plagues that Galen narrated, in *On Simple Medicines* 10 and *On the Usefulness of Parts* 3, were small, about which he writes that one was cured by human urine and the other only attacked feet.[108] In this rank, we can also place the plague of Verona that occurred in past years and which attacked these regions in 1555.

The medium one, between intense and weak quality of air, is when not as many people die as in a great plague nor as few as in a minor one. I think that nearly all plagues recounted by Hippocrates were medium, since there is no mention of great destruction and since he set down one or two examples of them for us in which they died on the third day, which also happened in Constantinople under Emperor Leontios, which was a medium [31] plague, in which it was written that 40,000 people died from plague.[109]

Therefore, I am of the opinion that the plague that afflicted our regions in these times must be placed in this middle rank. I am persuaded that it must be considered this because of comparisons with other plagues. For, I find in the greatest plagues either half or at least a third of the population died. Moreover, it was observed in these extraordinary plagues that barely one out of a hundred of the sick survived; in our plague not even a fourth of the population was wiped out (I speak about the cities where it struck, not the country homes). Furthermore, those who were occupied with curing the sick at this time readily recognized that out of a hundred who were sick ten or even more survived. Therefore, our plague was neither one of the greatest, nor great. Not that it must be considered among the smallest, in that the symptoms were extremely violent and also many died. So, I think (unless I am wrong) that it is clearer than the midday sun that our plague was generated from a harmful quality of the air.

## Chapter 12: On the nature of contagion: it is carefully examined where and how a body communicates, to what, and through what

It remains now that we look at also how contagion fomented and increased the plague. In order that we are able to investigate it precisely, I think it is worthwhile to examine briefly and clearly the nature of contagion. And because we have no explanation of the nature of contagion either in the ancient writers on medicine or in the philosophers, it is necessary for us to hunt for it in the common conception of the people. I find that people assign the word contagion to three things at most. First, it is assigned to the contagious disease itself; it is also assigned to what is poisonous; and it is also assigned to [32] that communication of the contagious disease. We will try to evaluate the nature of contagion according to the last conception.

Thus, contagion is nothing other than the communication of a disease from one body to another body, a disease (I say) similar in kind. And when I say disease, you should understand a preternatural entity. And I will not dispute here that this communication is a kind of motion, whether sensible or insensible. And in every motion or communication four issues must be considered: first, what is communicated; second, the body that communicates; third, the body to which it is communicated; and fourth, the medium through which it is communicated. What is communicated or transmitted in contagion, without doubt, is something preternatural. And there are three kinds of preternatural entities: the disease, the cause of the disease, and symptoms. Clearly it cannot be thought that the disease itself is sent, because it would place the disease, as I will show, in an inanimate body. And it cannot be said that the symptoms are transmitted, since they always are a consequence of disease, like a shadow and a body. Therefore, it must be most certain that what is sent is the cause of the disease.

The cause of the disease tended to be of two kinds, one is incorporeal, the other corporeal. It is an incorporeal cause when contagion occurs through the communication of an unmixed and pure quality, such as when numbness is communicated from an electric ray through its stinger, for, then clearly the simple quality is communicated. I think communication of this kind, through simple qualities into bodies, never happens with diseases. I will not speak about poisons that are external to the body, but I will leave this subject for the most careful discussion of the most famous and excellent man, who just began a treatise on this.[110] Thus, the communication of diseases comes from corporeal causes.

The corporeal cause without doubt must be such that it can be moved from place to place. Now, solid bodies in no way can be communicated and cannot be moved from place to place, [33] but only a fluid and vapor or spirit can. Therefore, what is communicated will be a vapor or fluid. You know that it is told that a fluid is communicated in scabies by Aristotle, at *Problems* 7.4, and by Alexander, at *Problems* 2.44. For, these two famous philosophers, asking why dropsy is not contagious like scabies, say the reason why is that the fluid of dropsical patients is in the cavity of the body but the fluid of those suffering scabies is on the surface of the skin and it is persistent and adherent.[111] Contagion also happens through fluids in the French Pox, when through touching and vehement shaking the diseased fluid is transmitted from body to body. Could there also not be transmission through fluids in pestiferous contagion? It is possible without doubt because whoever should touch the ulcerated pustules clearly will contract the disease as a result of the adherence of that poisonous and putrid fluid. But mostly the transmission is just of vapor and spirit in pestiferous contagion. And Aristotle, Galen, and their followers recognized only this transmission in plague, as I will show in the appropriate place. Moreover, since vapor is not a simple body but mixed, and just as mixed bodies have at least three degrees of qualities, it must be thought that pestiferous vapor of this sort is endowed with three degrees of qualities; these qualities are very evident from their effects. For, it is known from the effects that this vapor putrefies and burns. It is known that it penetrates and adheres. It is also most clear that it kills. Therefore, we necessarily are compelled to assert that this sort of vapor is fiercely hot, is subtle because it penetrates, is persistent because it adheres, and is poisonous and harmful to the entire substance of our nature, since it not only slaughters but also slaughters quickly. We have now, therefore, briefly explained what is communicated in pestiferous contagion.

The body from which this kind of vapor is communicated is of two kinds. One is diseased, [34] that is, already infected by the plague; the other is the fomite.[112] But not always and necessarily is the pestiferous vapor transmitted by these two bodies, sometimes by one, sometimes by the other, and sometimes by both. What I said about the fomite is established only by the observation of more recent people, because it is difficult to find among the ancient physicians that they believed the plague is communicated by fomite. Our very Galen said that associating with those affected by plague is dangerous.[113] Aristotle said that plague is communicated to those who are near, which happens either through breathing or perspiration.[114] But, as I said, when I carefully looked for fomites communicating the plague in the writings of the ancients, I was not able to find anything. Indeed, later writers, who either interpreted the ancient writings or taught medical theory, all the way up to the time of our grandfathers, transmitted no explanation of fomites, as wondrously this topic for many centuries was either unknown or passed over in silence.

A diseased body from which this vapor is emitted can be nothing other than that body in which there arises a bubbling up and putrefaction. The explanation of this matter is very clear, namely, that if vapors are to be lifted up and transmitted, for no other reason can this happen unless heat stirs up the humidity and does it vehemently. By this action, exhalations, breaths, and vapors arise, just as we see in bodies left outside, in which many vapors are lifted up while the solar heat stirs up the humidity; when it either does not act or does so very weakly, no vapors are drawn out, or certainly extremely few. Therefore, a body from which a pestiferous vapor is emitted is a fervidly hot diseased body. There is no reason why you should think that this happens perpetually, in that, not always is there a burning in bodies corrupted by plague. But even if it is not apparent to the senses, if contagion must arise, it is nevertheless always necessary that some putrefaction is present in the body, on account of which vapors are lifted up, since it comes to be from a preternatural heat [35]. But I will discuss this topic when I will dispute whether putrefaction is connected to all contagion.

The body that receives poison from a diseased body and then communicates it to another is called a fomite of disease. It is necessary that this body has many characteristics. For first, in order to receive, it must be rarefied and loose; in order that it preserves, it must be the correct size and endowed without any extraordinary active quality; it is neither very cold nor vehemently hot; it must be a rarefied body as dense bodies do not easily take in vapors. It also must be the correct size since, as Galen famously teaches us at *On Simple Medicines* 3.23, all destructive agents, however strong they are, even when assumed within the body, cannot do any harm unless they have the correct size.[115] For this reason, he rightly said a one-hundredth dram of cantharides and a spark of fire do nothing. Therefore, those vulgar ones who think this pestiferous poison can consist of some kind of minimal particle, in my opinion, must be ridiculed. I heard, not without laughing, some physicians saying that some people have contracted the plague from touching little pieces of thread, which no one of sound mind ought to think, yet the masses often believe this. But, as Pliny said somewhere, man's innate desire for living is such that people contrive monstrosities and absurdities.[116] The body must neither be, as I said, very cold nor hot, because both of these qualities destroy these pestiferous vapors, hence every contagion is annihilated by fire. Also frost annihilates all contagion. For the same reason, iron, marble, and all metals cannot be a fomite, both because of their density and also because of their coldness. And those who refuse to touch coins certainly seem simpleminded to me.

Bodies that truly can host fomites are all those that [36] are listed (unless I am wrong) in Leviticus 13, where, when Moses spoke about the contagion of lepers, he listed fomites, namely, wool, linen, leather, and yarn.[117] We can add to these also wood that is not dense and has small holes. But what should we say about walls? Walls that are dense and cold do not seem possibly suitable for fomites. Nevertheless, physicians, correctly, have great concern about these. It is taught, also, at Leviticus 14, that lepers' walls should be stripped and coated with new plaster.[118] I would say that not all walls can be suitable for fomites but only those that are porous because of age and those that are not at all exposed to air currents. For, just as we see a kind of mold condense on the walls in enclosed places, which comes to be from vapors adhering to them, by the same reason it must be thought that in enclosed places these pestiferous vapors fasten themselves and tenaciously stick to walls.

The body that receives the contagion bears some similarity to the vapor itself and to the body from which it emanated. For all reception, as you know from the principles of philosophy, is through similarity, such that like readily receives like. But in addition to this, a body receptive to contagion must be alterable and incapable of resisting the contagion, hence inalterable bodies or those that are so strong that they easily overcome poison are not suitable for receiving contagion. Similarity, through which this kind of reception occurs, is either the result of a concealed quality or a manifest quality. The concealed quality that makes this similarity and suitability for receiving contagion is nothing other than a certain intemperance of the heart, through which it is easily altered and easily contracts. In this way, the adverse quality also makes a contrary effect in the heart. For, as I already taught, it is often seen that those ones who otherwise have a balanced and ideal constitution nevertheless are most easily contaminated by contagion for no reason except that [37] they carry this concealed quality in the heart. The similarity through the manifest quality is situated both in the manifest temperament of the body and in the condition and in other aspects that pertain to the state of the whole body. For this reason, as I said, hot, wet, relaxed bodies full of impure humors easily receive contagion.

From this, you can draw out two corollaries. The first is that it is no wonder if sometimes entire families are seen to be wiped out by contagion because they have among them this similarity either from a hidden or a manifest quality. The second is that, because of this, at times some people are not contaminated by those who are infected and that it rarely occurs that beasts are infected by people or people by beasts, since in all of these this similarity through which bodies easily receive contagion is lacking. The other medium through which contagion is produced, when it is present, is nothing other than the air itself. Just as it receives light, heat, odors, fumes and transmits them to other bodies, this air receives putrid and pestiferous vapors and transmits them to other bodies. I said, when it is present, because when contagion comes through mere contact, no medium is present, but the transmission of the poison occurs immediately from a diseased body into a different healthy body.

## Chapter 13: How contagion acts on a healthy body

Since so many things act together for the generation of contagion, it remains that we see how generation of this sort comes to be, that is, what the poisonous and putrid vapors do that causes disease in the healthy body. Girolamo Fracastoro, a man most worthy of all praise in our times, who first opened human eyes to understand contagion, was of the opinion that those vapors putrefy at once and in no other way do they kill except through [38] extreme putrefaction.[119] But I am of another opinion: that those vapors not only kill by putrefying but also by altering in the same way that many other poisons do. I am led to think this because often it is seen that people in pestiferous constitutions die without any sign of putrefaction. Indeed, it is confirmed by experience that the most lethal contagion of all is that by which people perish without any sign.

The way by which these vapors kill through putrefaction and alteration is that when the pestiferous vapor has first entered the body it destroys the innate heat; this is apparent because immediately its operations collapse. When the innate heat of the whole body, especially of the heart, is disordered and mixed up, the humors, deprived of protection from it, are exposed to the fiery and pre-ternatural heat. The heat emitted by that fervid vapor immediately putrefies by dissolving the humors. Sometimes it happens that immediately the innate heat is disordered and destroyed by the poison of an extraordinary vapor and the person dies without any putrefaction. It also happens not infrequently that the patient does not die immediately from the disordered innate heat but survives for a little, as time is allowed for the putrefaction to develop. And for this reason, it happens that some die more quickly, others more slowly, for just as the poison is more or less potent, so it is that they come to the end of life more quickly than the putrefaction develops. Whether spirits or only humors putrefy in pestiferous contagion is an old and long disputed question. Yet, I am of the opinion, as I have shown elsewhere, that also spirits putrefy in a certain manner. So, you know how the pestiferous vapor kills in this manner both through alteration alone, like other poisons, and through putrefaction.

## [39] Chapter 14: Six most splendid problems about contagion are presented and solved

Now in order to finish the discussion of contagion it remains that I solve six most splendid problems for you here. The first is whether a fomite can ever transmit this disease-bearing cause to another fomite and then the fomite onto something else. For example, let underwear, which a body affected by plague has touched, be infected; the underwear is placed with other linen garments. The question is whether this underwear can infect other garments such that these garments, once infected by the underwear, can infect either other garments or people themselves.

To understand this is greatly relevant to public health and revealing common mistakes. The second is whether a disease-bearing cause can be preserved for a long time in a fomite. About this you will hear wondrous stories, since there are many who say that infected garments preserved and communicated plague after one or two years. The third problem is whether poison can be preserved in a fomite without harming that body to which the fomite is attached. So that, if someone has infected clothing and wears it every day, it is worth asking if in that clothing the plague can be preserved without harming that person. The fourth is why does it happen that some plagues are more contagious, other less, some corrupt animals, some a particular kind of person and particular places. The fifth is why putrid fevers are not contagious. For, it is also most evident from those bodies that suffer from putrid fever that the putrid vapors are lifted, although it is not advanced by any writer and it is not confirmed by any experience that putrid fevers are communicated to others. The sixth and last is whether contagion brings more destruction from direct contact, from a fomite, or from air.

For the solution of the first problem, I stipulate that a fomite is a body that is either alive [40] and has sensation or is inanimate. If it is alive and sensing, without doubt it can contaminate and convey another fomite. The reason is because sensing bodies have both an internal heat and movement. Thanks to the heat, the putrid vapor can be shaken and transmitted into another body; by means of the movement, the same vapor can be cast into another body. Accordingly, those, who think that dogs, cats, and other infected animals can sometimes also communicate the poison to clothing and other objects, do not judge poorly. If a fomite is an inanimate body, either it is agitated or remains still. If it is agitated, the explanation is the same as for the sensing body, namely, thanks to this agitation the poison can be communicated to other bodies. If, however, these infected fomites remain still, either they remain still enough that they do not grow warm or they grow warm. If they do not grow warm, my opinion is that they cannot infect other bodies because with respect to neither the agent nor the recipient is an action exchanged. It is not exchanged from the agent's side because that vapor is inert, powerless, and tenaciously affixed; it is not from the recipient's side because this clothing has no attraction by itself, and therefore, since neither can the infected body be emitted by itself nor the receiving body attract by itself, no communication and no action can come to be. For this reason, in my opinion, those who think that infected clothing can indiscriminately infect other clothing are most gravely mistaken. But if at the same time the clothing remains such that it grows warm, without doubt what is infected can infect another because the heat thins out the vapor and agitates it; consequently, it can be transmitted from place to place. But you will say, how can this clothing grow warm? Because of compression. For, the internal air, having been compressed, not only sometimes heats up but also ignites. The great Hippocrates said, in *On the Nature of the Child*, that he had seen with his own eyes Dorians' compressed clothes catch fire. Whether these Dorian clothes in Hippocrates are leather, [41] as some thought, or these clothes are linen, which Herodotus mentions, in book 5, this question does not demand to be investigated carefully.[120]

For the solution of the second problem, I stipulate that a fomite is either blown about or it is not. If it is blown about, as it happens either from the wind or from something artificial, there is little doubt that the pestiferous vapor cannot last for long. But it is necessary that it is destroyed by circulation and straightaway it is obliterated. And in regard to this, our predecessors must be praised, among others Marsilio Ficino, who taught in the book on plagues that clothing and walls are purified from all contagion in twenty days if they are aired out and cleaned.[121] If, however, a fomite is not blown about in any way, clearly the pestiferous vapor in it can be preserved for a very long time. For, if diseases are preserved for a long time in the human body, so much the more can they be preserved in bodies that lack a soul and sensation. The proposition is demonstrated by the opinions of the weightiest authorities. Hippocrates, in *On Internal Diseases*, writes that there is a certain disease in the left vein that is preserved and lurks in bodies for twelve years such that when it erupts it induces dropsy.[122] The noblest philosopher Theophrastus, in *History of Plants* 9.16, most clearly teaches that a preparation of poisons can be given so that for three or four months they remain in bodies without harm.[123] What should we say about the bite of a rabid dog? Galen's and Avicenna's opinion is that this kind of poison is latent for six months and even a year in the bodies of those who have been bitten.[124] And Albertus Magnus, in *On Animals* 7.2, testifies that he saw this kind of poison preserved in a body for twelve years and then it erupted.[125] Indeed, Albucasis, the most famous physician among the Arabs, recorded for posterity that he also had directly experienced that this poison of a rabid dog was concealed within bodies for forty years.[126] So, if the poisoned matter is preserved in a human body for many years, pestiferous vapor can be [42] preserved in a fomite for much more.

The reason for this is that in the human body poison always has an enemy that contends with it: the innate heat and the body's governing nature. In a fomite, pestiferous vapor and poison do not have any adversary; [the fomite] does not have heat or a nature that weakens it. Therefore, (unless I am wrong) it can be apparent enough through this demonstrative argument that it is not beyond reason that this pestilential decay is preserved for a long time in a fomite.

The explanation that Fracastoro used also is in agreement, that odors, stenches, and fumes are conserved for a long time in bodies, which is completely verified by experience.[127] Thus, it is not beyond reason that also pestilential vapors can be preserved. From this solution you can infer that it is most true what Evagrius writes happened in that greatest plague, in *Ecclesiastical History* 4.28, that, often healthy people, descending from infected regions and arriving in regions free from disease, infected those regions and the healthy ones there.[128] Therefore, preserving the pestiferous poison within themselves, just as if in fomites, they communicated it to others and, infecting the air, they introduced the plague.

To the third problem, I respond that the pestiferous poison can be preserved in excrement and people's garments without harming them but in no way can [be preserved] in living particles. I confirm this because, if it is preserved in living particles, vapor is either efficacious, or inefficacious. If it is efficacious, when it is in a hot body, without doubt it will harm with respect to the agent and with respect to the recipient. However, if it is inefficacious, it will not act on any living particle, so, it will also not act on those nearby. But if you object to me, that elsewhere I taught that a woman can communicate the French Pox to another person even if she is free from it, as if the woman preserves that French Plague and communicates it to others without being harmed from it herself, I reply that still now I say it is just as was established in our treatment of the French Disease [43] but there is a big difference between pestiferous vapors and that French decay, because in the pestiferous decay there is no rubbing and there is no action with respect to the agent or the recipient that is in the French Disease. Since it is acquired through intercourse and the woman's heat strongly agitates and the man's heat most strongly attracts, it comes to be that the French poison, although inert and powerless, is nonetheless communicated because of that violent contact.[129]

The fourth problem was why plagues are contagious for some and not for others. We have the solution explained in Lucretius' *On the Nature of Things* 6 and also in Fracastoro, who say, in the plague, various and diverse seeds move about, which are either amicable with these ones or those ones or hostile and thus sometimes affect this one and sometimes that one.[130] But Hippocrates seems to us to have discussed this problem more illustriously than everyone, in *On Breaths*, when he said that the same things are not beneficial and detrimental to all kinds of living creatures; but one body is different from another body, one nature from another nature, one nutriment from another nutriment.[131] As a result, it is no wonder, if plagues are not contagious to everyone in the same way, since the congruity and incongruity of the *miasmata*, or miasmas, is not the same in all regions or for all people, but a friend to one can be an enemy to another and vice versa.[132]

For this reason I am led to think it is true what Evagrius and Nicephorus Callistus write, namely, that during that most severe pestilence some were infected only by a glance within their homes, others, who hoped to die, were unable to be attacked by the plague even when they conversed, passed time, caressed, and even slept together with those affected by the plague.[133] In the same way, we can also understand why in that plague that Dionysius Halicarnassus narrates, in *Histories of the Romans* 4, only virgins and pregnant women were overcome by the plague and also why in that [44] plague that raged during the time of the physician Gentile [da Foligno], no women, as he reports, were infected but only robust men.[134] Of course, this happens because of this incongruity and congruity of the contaminations or of the occult property of a healthy person.

Why putrid fevers are not contagious was the fifth problem. Fernel attributes the cause to the secret property of pestilential fevers.[135] But beyond this property, there seem to be manifest causes. For, matter through which contagion arises in fevers has two main characteristics. First, it is maximally putrid and, because of the putrefaction, it is also viscous and sticky. And next it is so hostile and adversarial to human heat that it directly weakens until it is not strong enough to resist. Therefore, when vapors lift up from this putrefying matter, because of their viscosity they tenaciously stick and attach to the bodies of those nearby, and they blunt the innate heat so that it is not possible to resist them. The matter of pestilential fevers lacks these characteristics, for it is not maximally putrid, since its vapors are not so clingy and sticky, and it did not overcome and defeat the innate heat so much that it is unable to resist. For this reason, even if putrid vapors are emitted from the bodies of those with fevers into others, since they do not stick because the innate heat of the healthy resists and dissipates them it happens truly that they are not contagious and they do not give birth to a similar disease in healthy bodies.

For the sixth and last problem, I think it should be answered that, in and of itself, the worst contagion of all is that made by direct contact; next, that brought through the air; and less than the others, through a fomite. The reason is that in the first way, not only the touched part but also the perspiration and exhalation of the entire body attack, since those who touch those affected by plague necessarily are also exposed to these. But a fomite—since it does not have recent pestiferous vapors but those deprived of the heat of a diseased body and much weakened by time and thus inefficacious—[45] is without doubt apt to incur much less damage than air, which carries the fresh seeds of plague, still hot and therefore powerful, and continually plants them in the body. And our opinion is not opposed by the fact that the vapors with an attached fomite are stickier and therefore adhere more strongly, since the stickiness and viscosity are in no way active qualities; and although they can carry poison's great secret faculty, nevertheless, the poison affects more powerfully whenever it is tied to some active quality, especially heat. It is just as evident in medications as in poisons that they are much more efficacious when they enter a heated body. Experiences attest no less to this truth, since countless people, among us and especially foreigners, use mattresses, clothing, and other infected things with impunity. Much fewer are not contaminated, however, who draw within themselves air dirtied by vapors emanating from diseased and pestilential bodies or touch the infected bodies themselves. This is perhaps the true reason why very few historians and almost no physician, Greek, Latin, or Arab, left any mention in writing of contagion by fomites until our grandfathers' time.

## Chapter 15: What ways the contagion functioned in the plague of Venice and Padua

Since these solutions have been established about contagion, now let us see how it was at work in this plague besides the air. We said that contagion occurs through direct contact, through a fomite, and through air. In our plague, contagion carried out the massacre in these three ways. First through contact, since there is no doubt very many were afflicted, who, impelled by familial love [46] and mercy, cared for the sick with their own hands. Nicephorus Callistus, in *Ecclesiastical History* 6.20, and Saint Cyprian, in *On Mortality*, recorded for posterity that once Christians did this in that plague under Maximinus or the Emperors Gallus and Volusianus, when other peoples, as they say, abandoned their own children and brothers.[136] Therefore, as I said, there is no doubt that this contagion created many afflictions through contact. It also must not be doubted that fomites contributed much for causing this calamity, since very many infected things moved from here to there, which, having been touched and handled by healthy people, infected them. Appian of Alexandria, in the *Illyrian War*, put down for posterity that this happened, when he writes that the Celts, long ago, when they had subdued the Illyrians, having seized their things, were infected by the plague since the Illyrians had suffered from the plague.[137]

But, as I think, the contagion worked most of all through the medium of air, since this kind of contagion touches very many simultaneously and not just many but also most severely and powerfully. And the ancients knew about, or at least passed down to us, only this contagion, as I taught you earlier. The reason why more are killed by this contagion than by contagion through a fomite and contact is because, since the sick continually breath out pestiferous vapors and since infected spirits continually are emitted from their bodies, all of these are most readily dispersed throughout the air and very rapidly enter into other bodies, to which that air is necessarily continually attracted. Consequently, you can easily understand the true explanation of why whole families sometimes are wiped out and why, just as is confirmed by experience, the affliction creeps from one home to the next, namely, that when someone dies of plague in one home, the air is infected, which, drawn toward healthy people, then infects them. And this then happens more when the houses are narrow with small bedrooms since, because of their being closed up and of small size, the air is completely filled up readily [47] with pestiferous vapors. For, if, among the ancients, just as we read in the writings of the Jews and also in Hesiod, it was forbidden to stay in the bedrooms where menstruating women were cleansing themselves since they feared that the infected air could infect the men, how much more ought we think that it is dangerous to stay in those domiciles in which some people were seized and killed by the plague?[138]

Since the contaminations creep from these domiciles to those nearby, also the streets and entire cities are easily contaminated. For this reason, it happens that cities and towns are depopulated more than country estates, especially those cities whose streets are narrow and closed up. And perhaps in this matter the Emperor Nero deserves some praise, if he ordered that Rome was to be burnt in order to remedy the unhealthiness caused by the narrowness of the streets and lack of sun. Although, as Tacitus writes, in *Annals* 15, many believed the old layout of the city was healthier.[139] We understand, therefore, that in this plague the contagion harmed through contact, fomite, and above all through the medium of air.

## Chapter 16: The reasons for denying that the air contributed nothing toward causing this plague are brought forward

However much all these things are true, nevertheless, there is no lack of the most distinguished men in Venice and Padua, who are of the opinion that only one kind of contagion was at work in this plague. They concede outright nothing to the air itself. They want that it contributed nothing to causing this plague. Indeed, they deny that contagion through air had any significant role but only contagion through contact and fomite. In order to maintain this opinion, they use various arguments and also various experiences. The first argument [48] is that this continuous humid and hot intemperance, that of Auster, was not seen in the air, which physicians write makes the plague from the air. They say that the air did not appear so cloudy, so thick, but rather calm.[140] Dead aerial animals were not seen, as can usually be seen where there is that air that causes plague.

Second, they argue that if the air were the origin in some way of this plague, then, since the air is a continuous body, there must also have been a continual contamination of it. Therefore, since Venice and our city were infected, necessarily also Vicenza, Treviso, and all the suburbs of Padua ought to have been infected, which we know did not happen. In truth, they say it is confirmed by experience that the places closest to those that were affected by plague were completely immune. And it should not be thought that suitable and predisposed bodies were lacking at Vicenza and Treviso, which would have been attacked by the plague if their air had been infected.

Third, they argue that if the plague had come from the air, since there was this maximal poison in bodies, the maximal poison must have been in this air. And if it were maximal, the slaughter necessarily would have been much greater and much more widespread. They contend that the poison in the air must have been maximal since the principal causes are always greater at the start. Where poison comes to be, it is always greater in that body where it is first than in that [body] to which it is communicated from the first [body], just as they tell of the poison of a rabid dog, that it is maximal first in the dog and less powerful in the person who was bit by the dog. If the rabid person bites someone else, in the third person, the poison is then much weaker. Therefore, with this example they say, since the pestiferous poison in people was great, if it had been communicated to them by air, in that air it would have been very great.

To these arguments they also add many experiences. First, not only cities, but also all families and all farms were saved from this widespread destruction [49] that guarded themselves most carefully from contagion from fomite or contact. Moreover, those monasteries and hospitals that abstained from contagion through contact and fomite were immune from this calamity. Furthermore, they say, almost all who were seized by the plague have been found to either have had habitual contact with infected people, touched some infected objects, or met some other occasion for contagion. What is more, in Padua, Venice, and these regions, many were discovered who suffered from other diseases—tertian fever and continual fever—so that, if there were a defect in the air, these bodies that suffer other diseases would have been attacked more strongly by the plague. Lastly, they say that it is clear that the plague was first brought to Venice by some man from Trent, who gave rise to the possibility of contagion from infected objects.

And then, after the disease was nearly laid to rest, it broke out again when these infected objects were brought by someone else from Venice, and then, from there the contagion was spread.

## Chapter 17: The response to the above arguments

This is what has convinced many to think this pestiferous constitution was born only out of contagion. In order that we reply to their arguments, before anything else, it must be repeated that in any plague more always fall ill and die from contagion than from a defect of the air; and this can be confirmed from the fact that, when the constitution is very hot and dry or is strongly intemperate in some other way, even if it is extremely capable of altering bodies, nevertheless much fewer fall ill than in a pestilential situation for no other reason than that there is no contagion. Now, in the first argument they said that there was no apparent intemperance of the air, which is necessary for generating [50] plague. As I taught elsewhere from Galen's opinion, at *On Temperaments* 1.4, some pestilences are great, others minor.[141] In order that a great pestilence comes to be, it is clearly necessary that all the seasons of the year are intemperate, namely hot and humid. In order that a minor one comes to be, it is enough that one season of the year is intemperate, like the example of Cranon that Hippocrates laid out for us, in which the constitution only during summer was extraordinarily intemperate.[142] Therefore, since we had part of the summer and all of autumn characterized by Auster, as I said before, why should we deny there was some occasion [for plague] in the air? In fact, also the seasons before summer were unstable and did not keep their own nature. And although in these seasons no plague was formed, nevertheless, it started when seeds appeared.

But let us concede that until then there was no manifest intemperance of the air. Is it not clear—as Fernel, a physician of the greatest authority, contends—that, because of the heavens' occult powers or the earth's vapors, plagues also arose while the air is serene?[143] Therefore, since we also established that some harmful quality was fixed to the air, their argument is not valid at all against us. Much less valid is that no dead aerial animals were seen, that that darkness and turbulence of the air was not seen, since these signs imparted to us by observation alone must be searched for only in a great plague when the air's quality is intensely destructive. But now we assert that this hostile quality was not at all intense but medium, therefore, their arguments are weak. You shall look at, I ask, Galen, at *On the Differences of Fevers* 1.4. With this argument, he says that he foresaw and predicted future plague, not from the disorder of the air, not from dead animals of these kinds, but only from the fact that carbuncles spread and that the population was attacked by the same disease.[144] These are the most reliable signs needed for foreseeing [51] and recognizing plague from the air. Therefore, it cannot be doubted for this reason that our plague arose from the air and in particular from air tainted by the heavens. For, when I consider those wondrous effects, which, as you know, I saw with my own eyes, which I handled with my own hands, I cannot but ceaselessly affirm that this disease is truly divine.

To their second argument, I respond that all air is continuous with itself, but it is in no way necessary that, when one part of the air is contaminated, all the air is contaminated simultaneously and at once. For, if this were true, it would necessarily follow that in all plagues the earth's entire orb must be attacked by plague at the same time, which has never been recorded by anyone, as I will also demonstrate with examples. There are two most powerful arguments for why it is not necessary that all air becomes contaminated together simultaneously. First, because celestial powers are also received in different modes, which no one doubts. For this reason, it must not be denied that the air can be contaminated in this manner in accordance to its different parts.

The other reason is because, as I said, the air is also corrupted by terrestrial vapors. But exhalations of this kind are pushed here and there by the winds' force and by their own and consequently they corrupt sometimes this part, sometimes that part of the air. You have very splendid examples of this topic from rains, hail, and lightning, for, you will see sometimes hail beats down on one part of a village and leaves another untouched, just as for rain and all other meteorological phenomena, which happens for no reason but because different parts of the air are filled with vapors. If simple terrestrial vapors do this, what would stand in the way that also pestiferous exhalations, emanating from the earth, defile different parts of the air? But in addition to these, there is also the fact that in different parts of the earth, even those close to each other, bodies are found to be constituted in various ways. It is not because they say it cannot happen that [52] the bodies of those from Vicenza are predisposed in a different way than ours, since this can be both from that secret arrangement, which I spoke about, and also by a manifest one. For, Hippocrates writes, at *On Diseases* 4, and it is found confirmed by Theophrastus and Mesue, that one part of the earth differs from the part next to it with respect to whether it produces an abundant or scarce harvest.[145] If insensible bodies are constituted so differently, even from what is next to them because of the nutriment that they draw from the earth, one must not think it unreasonable that the bodies of those in different cities are predisposed and prone to receiving aerial impressions in a different way. Additionally, it is not true that Vicenza and Treviso were completely free of it, if in fact very often the plague began in those places, but the contagion was constrained right away through the vigilance of their leaders and was unable to expand at all. Hence, it is no wonder if these cities that avoided contagion were unharmed.

For, we also established that, besides the air, contagion has two modes, and these were evaded more easily by those who had only dangerous air than by those who had both air and contagion. And so that you will not think that I am delusional, I ask you to look over all the plagues described by writers. Never will you find that a plague attacked so that at one and the same time it assailed the earth's entire globe; rather always first one part was infected, then another. Thus, Philostratus tells that a plague in his era lasted fifteen years; thus, also Galen tells of a plague that persisted in his era.[146] Jacques Despars, in the commentary on Avicenna [*Canon*] 4.1 testifies that in his time, for five years, a plague overran the earth's entire globe and often villages and cities suffered with some villages unharmed. Not all cities were besieged at the same time, but through an interval of time, first one place and then another place were infected.[147] I ask that you look at the very plague recounted many times by me in Evagrius, the ecclesiastical writer. [53] Among other characteristics that he writes it had, he presents this one: that neither at the same time, nor with order did the same plague attack the regions, but without any order it struck like lightning, sometimes this region, sometimes that one.[148] Furthermore, often it was seen that in a particular city, half the population was infected and the other half was free from it.

Therefore, if these arguments are on hand, if there are most trustworthy examples that support that in other plagues caused by infected air the plague was not continuous but indiscriminately various cities were troubled, why must we deny that this plague arose from the air because Vicenza, because Treviso did not have the plague? In fact, also the countryside near Venice and near Padua was free from it, and this must not be denied in any way, since it does not lack an explanation, as you know, and there is no lack of very famous examples. What Thucydides tells is much worthier of wonder, that while the Athenians' city was suffering from the plague, the enemy, who devastated the fields beyond the walls with sword and fire, did not feel it, and also that the whole Peloponnesian was unharmed.[149] To these I want to add what Elia Capriolo recounts in *The Annals of Brescia*. During that most famous plague in Galen's time that vexed all of Italy under the Emperor Marcus Antoninus, Brescia and all its suburbs were unharmed, when nevertheless the plague was in all regions of Italy.[150] Matteo Villani says the same thing about Milan, which in the year 1348 was nearly unharmed, when Italy and all of Europe suffered from that most savage plague of all.[151] Indeed, there are no lack of examples of peoples who are found to have never been attacked by the plague, as is told about blacks and the Muscovites, and, as Pliny writes at [*Natural History*] 2.96, the plague was never suffered at Locri and Crotone.[152]

Here is their third argument: if the plague comes from the air, since this poison is great in humans, it must also be very great in the air, and therefore many more animals [54] and kinds of people ought to have died. I said and (if I am not mistaken) demonstrated most clearly that the air can never become poisoned in the same way as the kinds of poisons that animals use for self-defense. Indeed, it happens that air can provide the opportunity and be the cause for generating poisons in predisposed bodies. For, Galen, at *On the Faculty of Nutrition* 2.6, advising that fruit should be avoided, says that a foul humor accumulates from them in the veins, which, when some opportunity, even a slight one, is taken, induces pestiferous diseases.[153] Thus, it does not stand that this great poison in a person, therefore, must be very great in the air, because no one doubts that under the summer's air, feverish heats are generated in the human body, which are maximally hot, yet it does not therefore follow that there must be a much greater heat in the air. For, Galen said, at *On the Usefulness of the Parts* 8.2, that however hot the external air is, it is always colder than the brain, even though the brain is the coldest of all our body parts.[154] Indeed, this is true because at the moment when a poison is generated in the body, it is more powerful than what originates from it in another body; therefore, the example of rabies does not support their argument. In fact, I should say that for a rabid dog, among medical writers it is clear that this kind of poison is produced from the air's excessive heat. Must it be inferred consequently that therefore this poison of a rabid dog is much greater in the air? Absolutely not. Hence, the real reason can be adduced for why greater destruction in all plagues always comes from contagion than from just the air, namely, the poison generated in a person is much more capable of destroying than any defect in the air, on account of its size and efficacy and its capacity for acting and being affected, which is greater between the pestiferous vapors exuding from a body and the healthy body itself than what is between the [healthy body] and the air itself.

What they then say—that those cities and those people, who separated themselves from others, avoided contagion and were free from plague, and for this reason [55] it is a most evident sign that the plague was created from simple contagion—truly is a quite weak argument, unless I err. For, is it a valid argument that if Aristotle, not walking, does not teach, therefore not walking is the cause that Aristotle does not teach? Not in the least. This is the argument of people who are completely devoid of logic. For, closing themselves at home or somewhere else, they separated from the general association with people. Indeed, this is rightly done, in that, they were immune for many reasons, as they avoided contagion and also since they breathed less air than others. Whoever walks, works, or is occupied in business clearly becomes hotter than others and therefore necessarily draws in more air. And you should not think I am dreaming this up. Seneca, a most profound author, at *Natural Questions* 6.27, says that sheep are attacked more by the plague since they abundantly drink water under the open sky.[155] But of greater importance is that the great Hippocrates, who knew and taught everything, at *Epidemics* 6.7, tells of a certain constitution of air in which people frequently were attacked by coughing and catarrhs.[156] In this instance, he says that women were harmed less than others as they left home less often than men.[157] Will you say this happened because they avoided contagion? Not in the least, because that disease was epidemic but not contagious. This, however, happened because they drew in less air, since they left home less often, and therefore were infected less, just as also happened in our plague to those who kept themselves at home.

This argument is much stronger. Many who avoided contagion with every effort were seized by the plague, therefore, it is a sign that it came to be not just from contagion. We are witnesses, if we are trustworthy, and not only other highly respected physicians at Padua and Venice are witnesses but also the noblest men, who tell you that so many kept their distance with every effort from all contagion and yet were attacked by the plague. [56] Even though certain ones recognize the weakness of their argument, they say that those ones either do not wish to admit or disregard their contagion; and, what is worse, to be able to defend their opinion they seek at such length occasions for contagion that surely it would be necessary that those pestiferous vapors were made of steel if they must have persisted travelling on so many fomites. I ask: how do these ones expect to be trusted when they want to prove that all plagues are born from contagion and do not want to believe those who say, who swear, that they contracted the plague without any occasion for contagion? I appoint you the judges of this question. During that year, it often happened that when different cities were infected by the plague, on one and the same day two thousand persons in all of Europe were struck by the plague. Is it more likely that all of these people handled infected objects at the same hour or had some other occasion for contagion by which they were affected by the plague than that they all inhaled the same air at one and the same time? I ask that you evaluate and judge for yourself this reasoning.

In Venice, it is known through experience that almost on the same day all the neighborhoods of Venice were infected. Is this in agreement with the explanation that it happened because everyone handled infected objects at the same time or had other occasions for contagion or rather because of the shared air? But there must be a most evident argument about this question, namely, that those most prudent and wisest senators, after many attempts, decided to see whether it was simple contagion or not. And so, they locked down half the city in order to remove all chance of contagion.[158] Yet, experience teaches that, from the time the lockdown began, the disease grew so that they were forced to repeal the law.

What they say about monasteries and hospitals is most false, that they were immune, as they did not associate with others—if only it were true. At Padua, how many monasteries were infected, even among those who exercised the greatest care? We know the monks of Santa Giustina exercised every diligent care [57] in order to avoid contagion. And, yet, among them, those who were more careful than others died from the plague. The same thing happened to many others. I name those reverend fathers of Saint Anthony, some of whom I know were struck down by the plague not from their negligence but by a power sent down from the heavens.[159] Therefore, it is not true at Padua and Venice that the monasteries or hospitals were all immune, not to mention Milan, where, during this same time, the plague, having attacked, afflicted all convents, both for men and for women, more than anywhere else.

Nevertheless, should we concede this fact to them, still this argument would lack any examples and any reason, since Raymond, in *On Plague*, writes this happened in the region of Avignon when a greatest plague attacked through the air, namely, that the monasteries, prisons, and hospitals were immune from the plague, because those who live in monasteries do not draw in the air so freely and, therefore, do not receive as many celestial powers.[160] We can add another reason, that is, this type of person consumes the weakest drink, simple food, abstains from work, from sex, making their bodies not at all predisposed for receiving pestiferous destruction.

They say that it was learned from experience that whole families were wiped out only from contact. And I admit this could have happened and perhaps happened, for, I do not deny that contagion had a large role in this calamity, such that more died from contagion than from just the air. Nevertheless, it is not a valid deduction that many were truly infected only by contagion, and therefore, this plague was generated only by contagion. On top of this, they say that many were seen who suffered from another kind of disease in this city, in the suburbs, and in country homes that were close to those that were infected. I respond that this was indeed true but for very few. I say that very few fell ill with another kind of disease at Padua and Venice and in those places where the plague attacked. [58] Furthermore, among other signs I recounted this one to you, that very few were attacked by another kind of disease and that the other illnesses turned into pestiferous ones. But you will ask the reason why some are found to be ill from another disease when there is plague from the air. I already said that all bodies, as Avicenna taught, have some property that prepares it for the plague but another [property] for other diseases.[161] And Fernel used this reason most effectively to show that in pestiferous diseases there is a concealed and almost divine power.[162]

What will we say about the final topic on the origin of this plague, which everyone says was first brought by that man from Trent and then erupted again from the circumstances of some Venetian? I find that it has also happened in many plagues that the people, looking toward the earth rather than the sky, attribute the cause of the plague to some human condition. The Athenians, as Plutarch narrates, in the *Life of Pericles*, attributed the cause of that greatest plague to Pericles because by forcing much of the rural population inside the city he provided an opportunity for it.[163] Also, many thought that the plague that was active in the time in which Galen wrote *On Prognosis from Pulses*, *On Simple Medicines*, and the *Method of Healing* was carried into Italy by Emperor Lucius Verus, as Julius Capitolinus recounts.[164] In 1348, when that greatest plague invaded these regions, the people thought that the plague was carried to Padua by some Venetian, as those who wrote the chronicles of Padua at that time recounted.[165] Thus, if you look through histories, you will always see the people found some human event. For this reason, it is also possible that this man from Trent was infected and at the same time the seeds of pestilence began to be present in the air. For, it is likely that at the same time there were also many others infected from Trent in other regions but, nevertheless, they did not infect them because the air had not yet begun to be contaminated in those regions. As you know, there is a town called Piove di Sacco in the Paduan countryside, [59] where during that whole summer, Venetians and Paduans withdrew with every kind of furnishing and without any kind of protection employed, but the plague never appeared there, except around October, just when Auster dominated, which seems to be the clearest indicator that the plague began to spread there at the time when the air was infected.

But let us permit that this man from Trent gave the occasion for the plague, I say that it could have happened anyway that this plague (if it should be called plague) was only from contagion. For, it was very slight and did not enlarge, since whenever the plague comes to be only from contagion it does not expand very much and immediately retracts. And since at that time the most prudent Venetian senators applied every precaution, it was eliminated, perhaps because it was only a contagion, and for two or three months the city was completely free. In March it began again. And although these ones say that it took its opportunity from that Venetian, many say this is false. But, in my view, the argument is most convincing that, since, at that time the Venetian senate applied every precaution in order to remove the contagion, just like it had eliminated it before, it would have eliminated it so much the more if it had been only contagion, because now, having learned through experience, they were more careful and now the illness at the beginning was very weak and slight. Therefore, since they were most careful at that time, they turned over every stone, as they say, in order to abolish the contagion and it could not be done—in fact, instead, the illness apparently began to grow—the argument is most clear to me that this illness originated not only from contagion but from the air's imbalance.

I am not moved at all by that theory, which they present like it were the argument of Achilles,[166] that for physicians, hunting simply what is available to the senses, it is not at all relevant to investigate the hidden powers of the heavens or the occult influences of the stars, since I ask these ones that they peacefully decide [60] which physicians, whether recent or ancient, they wish to follow. On the one hand, I do not think the more recent ones would be embraced, since they have Fracastoro, Fernel, and many other physicians of great name, who easily refute them. On the other hand, there are those older ones, and it is appropriate to follow those legitimate fathers of medicine because of their incomparable experience and the authority acquired long ago. Thus, refuge must be taken in them. But now, it is clear that Hippocrates, Avicenna, and nearly all the Arabs most clearly counted the heaven's powers and influences among the causes of pestilence. But after they did not wish to adhere to these most reliable physicians, as is fitting, I ask that they show one physician among the ancients of any worth, who at any time put forward or thought either openly or obscurely that plague could come to be only from contagion, and right away I will gladly concede. Therefore, they should not use against us the argument that works best of all against themselves. It will be most pleasing to me that all the learned men see and carefully examine my explanations, because, since this topic is of the greatest importance, it will always be most welcome to me that the truth is found, if indeed the truth can be found in such a secret and divine matter.

## Chapter 18: Why and how the accidental symptoms that happened in this plague and others were formed

Having established and demonstrated the causes of pestilence in this way, now the path appears laid for discovering the reasons why so many and such great symptoms are seen in pestilence, just as we saw in our constitution. For, the pestiferous air, as Galen writes, at *On the Differences of Fevers* 1, or those putrid, pestiferous vapors carried by contagion within vulnerable bodies, first attack the heart itself, as if the citadel of our life, and, as they are [61] extremely hostile to life, they disturb the heart's innate heat, temperament, and entire condition and displace them from their natural order.[167] Then, necessarily the entrance of preternatural heat follows, which, heating the spirits and humors, makes fevers, as the heat is transmitted throughout the entire body. I say this happens for the most part because also sometimes people are slaughtered by the poison before there is enough time or a place granted for putrefaction and inflammation. And then sudden deaths occur without any sign or any symptom, like some that were seen in our constitution. It seems likely that it also happened in this fashion at Rome in the plague under Romulus, recorded by Dionysius Halicarnassus (book 2 [of *Roman Antiquities*]), in which, as Plutarch writes, in the *Life of Romulus*, and Zonaras, in *Annals* 2, people suddenly died lacking disease.[168] Jacques Despars, in the commentary on Avicenna [*Canon*] 4.1, in the chapter on pestilence, tells that in the pestiferous constitution that occurred in his time sometimes sick people came to him with urine [for him to inspect]; he touched them and found them to be without fever, without any severe symptom, yet they (he says) died immediately or right after they had left him.[169] This happened, as I said, because poison drawn into the body killed before burning and putrefaction could come to be.

When preternatural heat induces fever by dispersing humors, these kinds of fevers are either burning both inside and out, are tepid inside and out, or are burning inside but tepid outside. For, there are no fevers that are tepid inside and burning outside, in that in every fever the burning is always greater around the heart than in any other part of the body. For, the hearth and fuel of this fever is located around the heart. Pestiferous fevers that burn inside and out arise as the result of massive and widespread putrefaction, which not only burns the interior and is generated in large vessels but also spreads into the extremities and into all the smallest vessels. [62] Internally and externally tepid fevers come to be whenever the poison is much stronger than the putrefaction itself. Hence, you can gather that it is not always true, as some said, that pestiferous fevers originate from the most putrefaction, because, if this were true, it would be necessary for there to be the strongest burning in the body's interior. Yet, the authority of Galen, at *On Simple Medicines* 9 in the chapter on Armenian bole, and Avicenna's opinion, at [*Canon*] 4.1 in the chapter on pestilential fever, teach sufficiently clearly that this is not true.[170] Speaking about the internal and external heat, they write that pestiferous fevers often have a mild and gentle heat. Pestiferous

fevers become burning inside and tepid outside either, as Hippocrates says, in
*On Diseases* 1, because the wetness of the extremities dries out, since, once this
has been taken away, there is a lack of fuel for the innate heat and it is necessarily
diminished; or because, as Galen said at *Aphorisms* 4.48, since there is a great
burning in the body's interior, almost all the body's blood is pulled in and the
exterior parts, deprived of it, necessarily grow tepid.[171] Weak and frequent pulses,
which I mentioned, then follow these fevers: weak because the heart's powers are
dulled by the poison; frequent and short because of the need for refrigeration
and because of the burning. Sometimes also pulses similar to healthy ones arise,
as Avicenna said, because the poison but not the putrefaction affected the heart
most greatly.[172]

In these fevers, the heart's faculty always battles against the poisoned matter.
Then, very many severe symptoms arise from this battle, as you will see. If the
heart's natural faculty is overcome such that it cannot drive out the poison in any
way and cannot even attack, sudden death occurs without any sign, without any
excretion; they die as if struck down by God. If, however, the nature or faculty
of the heart drives out this poisoned matter, it either succumbs in the defense or
it overcomes. If it overcomes, the patients survive with some signs, as sometimes
there is a large outflow of blood, [63] sometimes excessive urine, sometimes a
number of carbuncles, sometimes buboes themselves. If, however, this faculty of
the heart drives the poison from itself but then is overcome, the patients die with
particular signs, which are various and different, as I will teach now.

Now, the poisoned matter that is driven out by the heart's faculty (take
notes on these so that you have something like a table of all symptoms before
your eyes) is either vaporous matter or humors. If it is vaporous matter, either
it is driven toward the head, which usually happens, or to other body parts. If
toward the head and it is full of phlegm, when dissolved, either these vapors
induce drowsiness or the dissolved phlegm, having been sent under the ears,
induces parotitis. If these vapors, otherwise bitter and fervid, strike the brain's
membranes, they induce headaches. And when they disturb the brain's temperament, they induce sleeplessness, sometimes dementia, deliria, and amnesia. And,
because they are mixed with the animal spirits and disorder them, they produce
paralysis. Similarly, these vapors, transferred to the ears or eyes, cause tinnitus
and problems with sight. If they are driven to the stomach, since they are poisoned and hostile to its nature, they cause nausea, loss of appetite, which sometimes are such extreme losses of appetite that there are many who would rather
choose to die than to consume food, as Galen said, in *Epidemics* 3.3.[173]

If humors are driven out by the heart's faculty, they are thick, burnt, and caustic, or thick and burnt but not caustic, or are subtle and piercing. If the humors are burnt, thick, and caustic, they make carbuncles, as this matter is driven to various different body parts. These carbuncles, if they are big and plentiful, are usually salutary; if they are small, so that the matter is little, they are more lethal. Also blisters and various ulcers arise from this matter. If the [heart's] nature drives out thick humors that are burnt but not at all caustic, [64] tumors usually arise either in the armpits, under the ears, and in the groin. And it usually causes larger or smaller tumors in proportion to the quantity of this matter. That pestiferous tumors come from copious burnt and thick humors you have the most trustworthy testimony in Procopius, *On the Persian War* 2, who, as I saw in a manuscript, tells that, in that plague, physicians, already having tried all remedies in vain, wanted in the end to investigate the nature of the tumors and, thus, found thick and burnt humors in the tumors after the cadavers had been cut open.[174] If the humors that are driven out by [the heart's] nature are subtle, they are ejected either separated from blood or mixed with blood. If separated from blood, they are ejected into the abdomen; Hippocrates said, in *On Diet* 1, that this cavity receives from all the body, like the sea.[175] If these humors are ejected through the bladder, the urine becomes copious, disordered, and cloudy; if through the stomach, there are fluxes, diarrhea, and dysentery, which many suffered in that constitution that Hippocrates recounts in *Epidemics* 3.[176] If through the mouth, raw, bilious vomiting happens; also worms are often expelled through vomiting or reflux, as was seen in this constitution. Worms, sometimes dead, sometimes alive, are thrust out by the poison's power not because they were generated at that time but rather had been generated before in the body. If subtle humors mixed with blood are driven out, they are either pushed upwards such that either drops of blood come from the nostrils, which are deadly, or great flows of blood, by which the ill often are saved. But if the humors mixed with blood are driven out through the skin, either they are little or a lot. If they are little, flowing out from the veins through *diapēdēsis*, that is, from those rarefied vessels, they make those small round spots. But if they are great, as Stephanus of Athens said in the commentaries on *Prognostics* 1.5, the small veins in the skins rupture from the excessive blood.[177] When these have ruptured, the blood under the skin stops, where they make these very wide spots—those welts that appear in both the living and the dead. But you had a very lengthy discussion from us about these kinds of spots last year.[178] However, I truly do not know the reason why Stephanus of Athens said in the cited passage that the sick with spots of this kind were called by Hippocrates, at *On Acute Diseases* 1.35, *blēptoi*, that is "stricken" or "castigated" by God, since in this passage Hippocrates is not speaking about spotted bodies of this kind but only of those who have a side of the torso spotted by pleurisy, whom he says were popularly called stricken.[179] Thus, you have the explanation and course of the generation of all accidental symptoms that happened in our plague and usually also happen in others.

## Chapter 19: It is shown through arguments and examples that it must be hoped that the Venetian and Paduan plague is completely wiped out and will not return again

It follows that we address the fifth subject, for which we promised to explain whether we must be hopeful for the future or fearful. For, as you know, a tremendous fear has invaded the minds of everyone that it should happen that, when the spring returns, this most monstrous savagery will lay waste to our regions again. And although Hippocrates wrote at the beginning of his medicine that judgment is difficult, nevertheless, it was the opinion of all philosophers and physicians that some power for foreknowing and sometimes divining future events is implanted in humankind.[180] Many tools are laid out by Plutarch, in *Platonic Questions*, and by Sextus Empiricus, in *Outlines of Pyrrhonism*, with which humankind can judge about the future and present, [66] which the Greeks were accustomed to call *criteria*.[181] But putting aside the philosophers' doctrines, let us use those tools for making this judgment that physicians were accustomed to use. There are two of these, namely, reason and experience, which Galen sometimes was accustomed to call the supports of medicine.[182] All reason is based on discourse; experience depends on sensation and examples. Above all, I want to lay out for you three [conclusions] in establishing this judgment. The first is that it should be expected that the plague will not return to our regions in the next years. The second is that in other cities and places that this plague has not assailed so far, the danger threatens that in the next years they are infected by this disaster. The third is that it will have to be discussed in depth if every opportunity for contagion should be removed with diligent effort in order that the vestiges of the illness, which otherwise would persist, are overcome and all danger lifted from our necks.

With these being stipulated, in order that I do not seem to have pronounced as if an oracle, I will try to demonstrate and prove with both reason and experience. If it should be dreaded that the plague will return, it must be feared because of the air, contagion, or bodies readied for the disease. It should not be feared on account of the air, because we clearly perceive from its effects that the celestial lightning that struck us is nearly totally extinguished. And the perceptible constitution of the present year is not the same as what can threaten us with a future plague through its nature. I say that the celestial lightning has nearly ceased in us because if in this time there seems to be some trace of the illness, its entirety is so small, so plain, so meager that it is nearly certain that it cannot derive from anything in the heavens but rather from contagion and human mistakes. It is within the power of almighty God to contaminate our air again. I do not deny this can happen. But as far as natural reasoning allows, it should rather be hoped that God almighty will use his kindness toward us, he who has been accustomed to use mercy after the whip.

[67] It should not be feared on account of contagion, since, if contagion would have made some extraordinary sickness, it would not be as diminished as it appears. I explain. Nearly three months have already passed from when this plague began to decline. When the people sensed this tendency, you saw how unrestrained they were, how freely they socialized right away, how they did not abstain from handling anything. Therefore, if it were to be feared from contagion, the sickness should have continued not diminished, as it was. What is more is that, as you will see, in other regions where the sickness was to continue, it never diminished. This is also a very powerful argument by which you can understand that this plague was not from pure contagion, because a great opportunity was given to it at Venice and Padua, nonetheless, as much as the opportunity was great, the sickness diminished. Therefore, if contagion could not have done anything so far to counter the downward tendency of the sickness, so much the less it should be feared for the future. Because sometimes by the power of the cold, by the length of time, all power of contagion is destroyed; sometimes because the most prudent men who are entrusted with the wellbeing of the city use every compunction for cutting off any opportunity; and lastly, sometimes everyone, having now learned well enough through experience, knows what skill and what carefulness they can use to save themselves from contagion.

It should not be feared for a property of vulnerability of bodies, as either all or most of those that had this property were killed. Moreover, there is the fact that this universal disease has its phases, just like all individual diseases, namely, a beginning, growth, stability, and decline. When these phases have finished, then the disease is said to be done, and this is very well known for any individual disease. Now, this universal disease had a long enough beginning, it had growth,

[68] its stability passed by, and it had its decline. Thus, it should be gathered that it is already finished, either totally or at least mostly. This can be confirmed by experience and examples.

It must not be denied that in many places the plague lasted two or three years. You have the example of the most famous Athenian one, which, as Thucydides narrates, in book 3, lasted for three years at Athens, such that the city was afflicted by nothing greater.[183] At Rome, as is in Livy, it also lasted for three years.[184] It is also told that at Milan the plague lasted for many years. This, I say, is most famous, but, as I have most carefully observed, only rarely when a plague has lasted for a long time did it have any significant remission but rather the sickness continued ever on, although it would have had some remissions, and this is clearly seen in Thucydides in the cited passage, although if there has been a great plague somewhere that significantly abated or terminated never, or extremely rarely, does it return.

You have examples of this matter at home. At Venice and Padua, often an extraordinary plague was active, but barely ever did it last a full year and once it left it did not return any more. In 1348, the plague began at Venice in March, it reached full strength in April and May, in July it began to decline, it was extinguished before the end of August, and it did not return any more. Indeed, Matteo Villani, the observer and chronicler of that plague, in *Histories* 1, writes that nowhere did it last beyond approximately the fifth month, even though he reports it was the most savage one of all since the beginning of the world.[185] In 1478, again there was a huge plague at Venice and in these regions. It began at the start of summer, it had full strength in the autumn, it began to decline in the winter, and then it ceased. At that time, that wisest senate began to form the Triumvirate for protecting health and to incinerate infected objects.[186] Again in 1528, this region was tormented by a greatest plague that lasted three or four months, enough for a massive number of people [69] to be annihilated. Yet, it ceased and did not return any more. In 1555, again there was a plague in these regions, although not remarkable; it ceased, and did not return.

I know that someone will say here: was there not a plague last year that seemed to have ceased after winter was over and nevertheless returned? I cannot judge, students, that this must be labeled plague in which barely two or three died in a single day. Perhaps, there were some kind of beginnings of plague, but it was not plague. If, therefore, in other pestilences it is observed that they never returned when people were not careful at all, or much less than now, how much more must we be hopeful that it will not return, when there is no lack of assiduity and compunction and many remedies are employed that were never in use elsewhere?

The reason is clear enough why it happens that once after a great plague has laid waste to some region, it does not return any more. First, because the heavens' powers are lacking, without which an extraordinary plague does not arise. Furthermore, the same thing happens in great pestilences that it is shown by experience that those who have suffered the plague once, as Thucydides recounted about his plague, and those who have suffered the quartan [fever] once are either not easily attacked or never attacked by it again.[187] Physicians assign a reason for this phenomenon, namely, that all the matter, which was the fuel of the sickness, is evacuated and consumed; with this consumed, nothing more remains that can rouse up a new sickness. For the same reason, it happens that those regions, once tormented by the plague are not attacked after they are freed from it, unless after many years, since all these bodies are consumed that had fuel in them and a vulnerability for the plague. Also, for this reason, those, who have been perfectly freed from the sickness by the long duration of the disease and the consumption of depraved humors, return from the lazaretto in better shape and more attractive. Therefore, the return of this sort of disease should not be greatly feared.

The reason why I should fear for those other cities and places that were [70] not yet tormented by this plague is this, because, when I think about the course of this pestilence, certainly I seem to see that this lightning bolt will run through nearly the entire globe in the same way it left us. For, in the past years, Constantinople was tormented, then the sickness crossed to Sicily, afterward to Trent, Verona, then Mantua, in that year Venice, Padua, and lastly Milan felt a loss of this kind. Transylvania, a large area of Germany, also was tormented. What is more, it crossed from the east into Sicily and from there into Italy, as also Matteo Villani recorded that the plague did in his time, which afflicted most severely almost the earth's entire globe and especially all of Italy.[188] With respect to this, that plague recounted by Nicephorus and Evagrius discourages me greatly, which, since it had all the same symptoms and same diseases that our regions experienced, it is such that I fear it will be similar also in this case. For, these writers recount that almost no part of the globe was untouched but some cities were nearly completely ruined; in others there was the plague but it went away immediately; in some many families were utterly destroyed; in others only one or two families were ruined, the others persevered unharmed.[189] They also add that there was something new in that plague, that some, leaving infected regions for healthy ones, were the only ones attacked by the sickness, but sometimes they also contaminated others. If you compare the whole appearance of that greatest pestilence and the other one described by Giovanni Boccaccio and Matteo Villani with ours, you will see almost everything happened.[190] The one remaining

thing that also makes ours similar to that one, is that it touched all cities, especially those that have a greater population, as Thucydides tells happened after
the Athenian plague.[191] Nevertheless, I earnestly ask the greatest God almighty
to relinquish this vain and ineffectual fear of mine.

## [71] Chapter 20: A treatment for the plague is proposed, and it is taught what princes and republics ought to do before the plague arrives

Since it is observed that medicine or any other human art can do nothing against
the plague, perhaps it would be more satisfactory, with its cure renounced, to
not detain you in vain, especially because it seems the nature of plague is such
that it kills most of the sick and yields to no remedies. As that one says "the cruel
calamity broke out on those who cure, and the arts harm its creators."[192] Yet, as
Marcus Varro said, in *On Farming* 1.4, even if healthfulness, which is brought
from the heavens and earth, is not in our power but in nature's, nevertheless,
there is much in us, since we can make what is very severe lighter through our
attentiveness.[193] Because of this and because of what I have already said about
the plague, I have decided also to include assistance against it. But since the
plague has a double aspect, one with respect to its being a common disease that
attacks the population, the other with respect that it concerns private citizens,
for this reason, one part of the assistance pertains to princes and republics, the
other part to any private citizen. Therefore, in order to discuss perfectly this
section, I will say first what protections are required of princes and then what
should be employed by each person. Some of what the prince must provide
against the plague must be done before it arrives, some while it attacks, and
some after it has gone away.

In all of these, they must always pay attention to three things: air, contagion,
and the vulnerability of bodies. Air, as you have learned, partly is corrupted by
the heavens and partly takes up the sickness from the earth. As for what pertains
to the corruption of the heavens, princes and republics must do nothing except
immediately take refuge in the greatest almighty God, the source of all mercy,
who alone can remove the air's corruption [72] from the heavens. Our Galen
teaches and almost all historians testify that our predecessors practiced this. For
the rest, the best princes and republics, first of all, must be vigilant so that all the
city's streets are most carefully cleaned; sewers (whose filth, Ulpian says, menaces

the pestilential sky with ruin), marshes, and swamps are purified; and whatever can give birth to stenches, putrefaction, or any mold are eradicated.[194] You have learned that from all these the air can be most greatly corrupted, so that, when this circumstance is removed, the goodness of the air can be most expected. For, [Diogenes] Laertius wrote in the life of Empedocles that at Selinunte he averted the plague that had attacked them from the stench of the adjacent river by having steered two nearby rivers into it at his own expense.[195] They also must be vigilant that only healthful winds are admitted within the cities. This can be done by obstructing the gaps in mountains through which pestiferous winds flow. For, in this way they say Empedocles saved his homeland Agrigento from the plague.[196] In order that the best winds are admitted, it must be planned that throughout all the city the windows that let in Aquilo are opened but those that admit contrary winds are closed and blocked. Marcus Varro tells that the island Corfu freed itself from an oncoming plague by blocking its windows that faced Auster and opening those that pointed toward Aquilo.[197] I told you that Austers carry plagues, as Pliny (*Natural History* 7.50) justly wrote that the plague always goes from southern parts toward the west.[198]

Princes must also be worried about avoiding contagion. Above all, they must watch out that no one comes from infected regions. You heard what happened in that plague recounted by Evagrius, namely, leaving infected [regions] and going to healthy cities, they frequently contaminated all of them. But whoever comes must be detained, locked up beyond the city for a while, until it is certain he is undamaged and [73] healthy. For the same reason, the greatest care must be heeded that no goods come into the city, especially those that I taught were fomites of plague. I truly do not think that the plagues of the past were so vicious and widespread for any other reason except that they had no, or little, concern for contagion, since not only did they not have any concern about infected objects but also they did not separate (as far as I remember) the sick from the healthy in any way. It is no wonder if today also some foreign countries are often attacked by the plague, since they are completely negligent in avoiding contagion, which you have learned always slaughters more in every plague than the air alone.

Princes also must be careful and worried about the predisposition of bodies and above all it must be taken care that the supply of grain is great so that the poor have enough to be able to sustain themselves. Indeed, Galen, Avenzoar, and many historians tell that plagues often arise for no reason except that the people, because of a lack of grain, are forced to feed on impure food.[199] I know that some of the noblest cities increased the amount of work for artisans, so that the people were fed, which certainly I can only greatly praise, since the people while they earn from the crafts also buy food for themselves without difficulty and do not secretly put together affairs in cities and suspect places in order to seek wages. Rotten fruit, rotten food must be completely removed from cities. Dionysius of Halicarnassus, in book 4 [of *Roman Antiquities*], tells of a certain plague that he said most severely attacked virgins, pregnant women, and boys.[200] Many believed it originated because bull meat was sold to the people; for this reason they write that the Taurian games were established afterwards.[201] No less care must be taken so that the water in cities is optimal and healthy, since, as Aristotle said, it is of the utmost importance which kind of water people nourish themselves with, since no food can be close to pleasing or useful without water. We know sometimes whole armies were wiped out by the plague [74] for no other reason than from foul water. And our predecessors, as Vitruvius writes at [*On Architecture*] 1.4, before they founded cities, they first examined with great care the waters of the places in order to be sure that also the people could live in health because of the salubriousness of the waters.[202] Brothels should be removed, all prostitutes should be expelled from cities, in that this is a great opportunity for the generation as well as for the growth of plague. Steam rooms should be completely avoided, since, because of the air and social interaction, these locations usually are very pestiferous, especially in these times. Jacques Despars tells that, during that plague, he took care that all baths and steam rooms were prohibited and consequently he was greatly cursed by bathers.[203]

The greatest remedy of all, which princes must apply at once when there is a suspicion of a future plague, is that all paupers, who live badly and maintain themselves badly, should be driven out of the city into healthy places where they can nourish themselves comfortably. For, it is agreed that this remedy was carried out at other times in Venice, as Sabellico narrates in *History of the Venetians* 4.3.[204] This remedy was greatly beneficial once in France; it was beneficial, as I learned, most recently at Milan, and indeed correctly, since the true and principal spark of plague is that people, commoners, and paupers—who, because of narrow homes and poor diet, are contaminated most of all—spread the plague most of all.[205] Also, in such times princes must allow the nobles to leave for the countryside, since cities are always more contaminated and more dangerous on account of that thick and closed-up air, corrupted by the vapors of the sick and the dead. The countryside is always safer. Plutarch writes in *Roman Problems* that the ancients had this custom such that they always built the temple of Aesculapius outside cities for no other reason than that the air of the countryside

[75] is healthier than in the city.[206] These should be all the things that princes and republics must do before the plague arrives.

## Chapter 21: What princes and republics must do while the plague is attacking and when it has just stopped, so it will not be revived

When it has already struck, many think the principal remedy is to alter and dry out the air with fire. Marcus Varro, Plutarch, Galen in *On Theriac*, and Aëtius tell that long ago Acron of Acragas and Hippocrates of Cos used this remedy but there was no lack of those who condemned this treatment.[207] And among them is Raymond, in *On Plague*, having been convinced by the argument that pestilential fevers are burning and, therefore, the burning should even increase from the fervid and hot air.[208] I think in this situation the greatest caution must be used. Certainly, during the winter and autumn, fire lit throughout cities can be of great use. But at the height of the summer's heat, either no fire or a mild one should be lit, perfumed with flowers and woods, just like Galen testifies that Hippocrates did.[209] For this reason, I cannot approve of those who in such times burn infected furnishings in cities, since not only is the air more inflamed but also there is the vilest odor. Because of those oppressive fumes, nostrils are irritated, heads are stuffy, and there are many sicknesses. I think this also greatly harmed this city because it seemed, when things were incinerated in the city, the plague worsened.

Cadavers must be carried out of the city with the utmost care and either carefully cremated—far from the walls and in a place from where the winds do not blow toward the healthy—or buried in deep ditches. Indeed, Diodorus Siculus (book 14) [76] writes that two things most strongly increased that plague of the Carthaginians: the stench of unburied bodies that no one dared to touch because of the fear of contagion and the putrefaction of marshy places.[210] Nor should those be believed who think these cadavers are not contagious since, even if they are cold to the touch, nevertheless, when they putrefy they are necessarily hot and fetid and pestiferous evaporations rise from them. This violently increased the plague at the start in Venice, as cadavers were kept unburied in the city and in their homes for many days because of the lack of gravediggers and because they were cremated in the old lazaretto, from where smoke and the pollution of the burnt bodies was pushed into the city by the wind.[211] It is told, among other things, by Thucydides that, in that plague, birds and carnivorous beasts did not touch the cadavers, since even these animals were taught by nature to avoid the contagion of cadavers.[212] You read in histories that many plagues grew because the cadavers were left unburied. Also, during this time care must be taken that all the city's streets are clean and without mud and rubbish. I recall reading in Lucian, in *The Scythian*, that the physician Toxaris once freed Athens from the plague when he ordered the city's streets to be cleaned and all the alleys sprinkled with wine.[213]

The greatest care must be taken for contagion. First, princes must make provision so that, if it is possible, everyone attacked by plague is removed immediately beyond the city into the lazaretto, where they can still be cared for attentively and with every Christian charity. Not only must the sick be carried away, but also all those objects, all furnishings, that could have been infected by the sick. Also, during this time, care must be diligently taken that no one steals these infected objects, so that if a patient having been taken away should die, all his possessions must be burnt as soon as possible. Nothing is worse than to collect these objects. But if the patient survives, care should be taken that these objects are cleaned in the same way that you can read was done for lepers in Leviticus.[214]

And, since often in the homes [77] from where the sick were carried away, there remain also some who are healthy, there must also be great concern to see whether or not these ones are able to survive in these homes. Because, if there is a fear that they can survive through some intervention, also these ones must be sent outside of the city, although separated from the sick, in places where they lack nothing needed for surviving the disaster. But if they should have large and commodious homes, it should be allowed that they remain in such a way that they do not go out for many days, nothing is carried out of the homes, and the assistance necessary for their survival is brought to them. It happens sometimes that also nobles and the rich are attacked by the plague, for whom it is not fair that they are sent together with commoners to lazarettos. Therefore, it must be provided that they leave for their own villas or they build wooden houses outside the city or, if for some reason they must remain in the city, it must be taken care that not only their homes remain closed and that nothing is carried away from them but also that these patients remain separated from the healthy with the help of a servant or even a physician. Indeed, this attention assists especially these nobles but also assists the whole city. For, by having applied these remedies, the possibility of the propagation of the plague is averted.

There were those who believed that, among all remedies, the strongest is that each person should remain closed-up at home for a fixed number of days and should not travel through the city. In fact, this remedy, as I heard, helped the Milanese. But it was ascertained that it was not helpful for Venice and Padua. I truly recommend that what I have proposed should be done more than anything

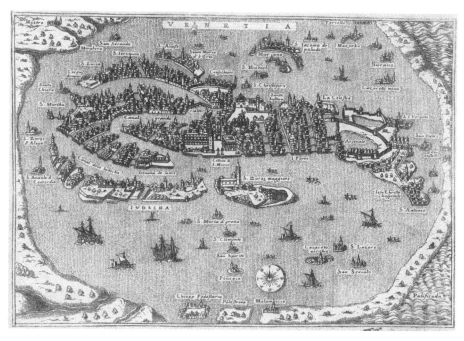

Figure 3. A view of Venice from above, a few years before the plague.
The Lazzaretto Vecchio is shown in the lower right-hand corner.
The Lazzaretto Nuovo is in the upper right-hand corner. The engraving
made by Girolamo Porro is found in Tommaso Porcacchi, *L'isole piu
famose del mondo* (Venice: Galignani & Porro, 1572). Courtesy of the
Wellcome Collections (https://creativecommons.org/licenses/by/4.0/).

else but I do not condemn this remedy since it makes these people use less
infected air: they do not work, they do not become hot, and they do not interact
with infected people so that this aid can be helpful. But unless two [rules] are
followed, this remedy can be lethal. One is that food suitable and fit [78] for the
poor should be administered; second, that it should be prohibited that many
live together in a single house at the same time. I said to you elsewhere that the
Athenians accused Pericles of having given an opportunity for plague by forcing
a great number of country folk to live within the walls. Livy also writes, at 3.1,
that under the consuls Lucius Aebutius and Publius Servilius a plague was made
at Rome because the people, forced into close quarters, lived in great numbers.[215]

Princes and republics must prepare the same things for the predispositions
of bodies that I said must be done before the plague. When the pestilence has

stopped, the princes' concern must not be any smaller for making sure the sickness does not return again. Therefore, above all, countless thanks to immortal God must be given. Every effort must be made with care that all streets are cleaned as much as possible. Often after the plague rubbish and bits of clothing and bedding, in which pestiferous vapors are preserved, remain in the streets. With equal diligence, all infected homes must be cleaned and, just as the ancients did in the home of lepers, if it is useful, it should be provided that walls are covered with new plaster. All suspect furnishing must be incinerated. Sabellico tells, in the last book of *The Histories of the Venetians*, that, when that plague had ceased its attack, in the end, those wisest senators burned innumerable furnishings that undertakers had collected from infected objects.[216] Without a doubt, it will be most useful if now the Venetians and Paduans employ that remedy. Take notice that, before those times narrated by Sabellico, it is not easy to find a record of infected objects having been incinerated at Venice or elsewhere. What the prudence and attentiveness of princes needs most is that they help those paupers, their parents, their relatives, and everyone deprived of wealth, who, returning from the lazarettos to the city, since they do not have anything to eat where they stay, not only frequently die but also [79] preserve the fomites of plague and perhaps can give an opportunity for the sickness to spring up again. Yet, I, dependent on the mercy of God and the suitable remedies of most prudent men, trust this will not happen, as I have said before.

## Chapter 22: How an individual should protect himself from the plague

Next, following our proposed order, we will now show the aids that private citizens must employ during the plague. Now, these aids come in two kinds: one for the healthy to use for preserving all bodies, the other to administer to the sick. Since all preventative assistance consists in removing the causes, above all the air must be considered. The divine Hippocrates' opinion, in *On the Nature of Man* 2, is that, where diseases arise from the air, nothing is more readily and easily changed straight away than air and location; afterward, what everyone says, emanated from the oracle of Hippocrates: "[go] right away, far off, [return] slowly."[217] Celsus understood the same thing, when, discussing the rules for protecting oneself from the plague, he said it is necessary to travel and sail.[218]

Among the older authors, there was disagreement about what kind of air one should travel to. Avicenna approved moving to thick air, as this kind of air putrefies with more difficulty.[219] But on this question, Avicenna was deserted by his followers, and rightly so. For, it is not true that thick air is immune from putrefaction, since it is such because of vapors and these are liable to putrefaction. Therefore, one must rather go to those regions where the air is pure and thin and where plagues did not usually attack or only rarely. If the air cannot be changed, one must [80] improve the air within the home. And because the air's defect can be in an occult or in a manifest quality, attention must be given to counteract both kinds of qualities. Usually the hostile quality of air is extremely hot and wet and, therefore, the air will be improved by cooling and drying remedies, which Avicenna understood, when he taught that rooms must be cooled.[220] Many methods for improving the air were discussed by the ancients. The most effective of these is to sprinkle bedrooms with rose water, rose vinegar, water of water lilies or sorrel water, and water of orange flowers. Rhazes also approved steeping hand towels and linens in vinegar and placing them on the hangings on bedroom walls.[221] Also, it helps to scatter citrons, quince, flowers, willow leaves, vines, rose flowers, and water-lily leaves on the floors, since all these usually improve corrupted air. Averroes, in the last chapter of *Collectanea* 6, approved costus, storax, and galbanum; he also approved terebinth, since it opposes the plague with a particular quality.[222] But, although all these are useful, much more useful and pleasant is to equip the home with some light and agreeable fumigation. When the season is hot, the recipe should be:

Rose water, 5 pounds
Rose vinegar, 3 ounces
All kinds of sandalwood,[223] 6 drams
Citron rinds, 3 drams
Camphor, 1 dram
Mix.

When the season is colder, this recipe should be more suitable:

Malvasia or scented wine, 5 pounds
Rose vinegar, 3 ounces
Rose water, 3 ounces
Cloves, 2 drams
Cinnamon, 2 drams
Mix.

[81] The way for preparing these fumigations is that they are all put in a small pot and held above coals in the bedroom so that they effuse fumes throughout the entire bedroom. I said what my opinion is about burning fires against the plague; consequently I cannot recommend that, in the summer, when the plague rages, there should be many fires in bedrooms but there should either be none or ones that are small, peaceful, from flowers or small pieces of aromatic wood. Indeed, it was observed in Venice, in that year, that many died who worked with crafts that use fire, such as blacksmiths or goldsmiths. And this was not without an explanation, since, having been rarefied by the fire's power, their bodies more easily admitted the air's contaminations.

Avenzoar, as Averroes also noted in the cited passage, among other things, recommended the scent of goat urine because of its property against the plague.[224] And in past years I went to Vienna for the well-being of Emperor Maximilian [II], and one day when I lunched with the most revered chancellor of Hungary, I saw a large goat kept in his rooms. When I asked what the reason was for doing this, he responded to me that it was for the plague. Thus, I noted that this remedy of Avenzoar was employed at some place also in our times.

But I approve more that pleasant smells be sought. Herodian, in book 1, wrote that, when Rome was struck by that greatest plague, under the advice of physicians, the emperor Commodus cut down Laurentum, where many forests of laurel were seen, since the odors of the laurels then were more valuable for avoiding the air's contagion than the pleasantness of their shade once was. He adds that, in the view of physicians in that city, many filled their nostrils and ears with the sweetest lotions and used perfumes and aromatics so that the sensory openings, filled with these smells, would block the corrupt air or overcome what had been let in with a greater power for a long time.[225] For this reason, it is often useful to wash the hands and mouth with rose vinegar or rose water. It is also useful to wear gloves, as they say, smeared [82] with flowers in the summer or anointed with musk and ambergris in the winter.[226] For this I also approve of those little balls carried in the hands, that should be made according to this recipe:

All kinds of sandalwood, 1 dram
Flowers of red roses, 1 dram
Myrtle,[227] 1 dram
Zedoary, 1 scruple
Scarlet grains or kermes, 1 scruple
Camphor, 5 grains
Musk, 5 grains

Galbanum, 3 drams
Labdanum, 3 drams
Make a ball with willow charcoal and oil of orange flowers.

In cold seasons, this recipe will be useful:

Aromatic reeds, 1 dram
Cloves, 1 dram
Mace, 1 dram
Germander, 1 scruple
Citron seeds, 1 scruple
Gentian, 1 scruple
Agarwood, 1 scruple
Dried styrax, 1 scruple
Myrrh, 1 scruple
Ambergris, 4 grains
Musk, 4 grains
Purest labdanum, 8 drams
Make a ball with clove oil and willow charcoal.

Whether it is better during this time to live at a high level or at a low place is generally found to be answered by physicians such that one should live up high when the air is contaminated by pestiferous vapors from the earth but in lower levels when the corruption is sent from heaven. In whatever manner, one must always flee [83] wherever a multitude of people congregates during this time. It is also greatly useful to avoid all suspected people and their places. Similarly, all clothing must be clean and neat. They should be changed often and kept in chests where there are various flowers and especially quince, citrons, or oranges. Indeed, our forefathers, as Theophrastus, in *History of Plants* 4.4, and Athenaeus, in *Deipnosophists* 4, testified, had no use for citrons except to mix them in with clothing to preserve them from all filth and putrefaction.[228] Leather and thin silk clothing are the best for everyone in this period. Wool, linen, cotton, and fur are all more dangerous since pestiferous vapors are easily taken in and retained by them. Consequently, also long articles of clothing should be banned. And perhaps so many physicians at Venice were killed because they saw patients with those broad tunics.

Sleep and wakefulness must be moderate. Beds should be clean and neat. It is most dangerous to sleep in the open or under trees whose shade is pestiferous. The body must be exercised moderately, and above all one must be careful that the body does not heat up in any way. For, it is Avicenna's most famous opinion, at [*Canon*] 1.3.5.1, that in this period one must strive for quiet and leisure in order to avoid the necessity of breathing in air.[229] And it is shown by experience that in these times those who worked excessively were infected. There were many who were seized by carbuncles, buboes, and fevers because of too much exercise. And I know many were killed in this way. All powerful motions of the soul should be kept distant, especially anger and fear, as experience establishes that the bolder are less in danger. Therefore, in this period it will be helpful to enjoy every kind of delight. I remember that I read in Plutarch, in *On Music*, that Thales chased away a certain Cretan plague from the Spartans [84] using only music; this mention of Thales is also in Pausanias, [*Description of Greece*] book 1.[230] I think that the music of Thales and of those soldiers, who chased away the plague with song in Homer, is nothing but hope, joy, and happiness, with which souls and bodies can fight more forcefully against pestiferous disease. If anything should be shunned in this time, without doubt, sex and bathing must be avoided. For, besides that the opportunity for contagion is present, it also renders human bodies more languid, rarefied, and relaxed and, therefore, they more readily draw in the pestiferous air.

But perhaps someone would ask here if it is bad in these times to rarefy and open up bodies. For, Galen, at *On the Differences of Fevers* 1.4, approves that in these times open bodies are unharmed, indeed, he adds that he was accustomed to doing this.[231] Therefore, it does not seem to be incongruous that bodies should be rare and relaxed, which Avicenna seems to have condemned.[232] This question made many interpreters agitated. But I was accustomed to explain the question in this way: there are two kinds of obstructions, as is pronounced most clearly in Galen's *On Simple Medicines* 5.12, namely, some are internal, some external.[233] In the time of plague, the internal obstructions must be completely removed, and care should be taken that all of the interior of the body is opened up, which Galen knew in the cited passage. However, he pronounces otherwise about the outside, for, during that time, the outside of the body must not be opened up because the infected air enters more readily and I think Avicenna knew this.[234] A soft stomach should be preserved; and if it is hard or constricted it must be softened either by a light clyster or by broths of mallow and beet. I have learned from myself and others that frequent use of bread that has a lot of bran renders the body relaxed. For this reason, country folk never suffer from a constricted stomach. And it was Hippocrates' opinion in *On Diet* that this sort of bread nourishes less but is more of a laxative.[235] [85]

Food and drink must be as moderate as possible and those who think one should eat and drink abundantly are greatly mistaken. I know many learned this at their own peril; and at Padua and Venice we saw that big drinkers, who thought that they would ward off the plague with generous quantities of wine, died. Rhazes, the greatest experimenter, at *For Almansor* 4, completely forbade wine in the time of plague.[236] I do not embrace his advice at all, but it is much better in the summer to drink sometimes water or light wine slightly diluted. In the autumn and winter, it is permitted to drink it unmixed. Cornelius Celsus set the rule that some water, some wine must be drank.[237] In place of wine, we have many drinks that are no less pleasant than useful: pomegranate wine, barberry juice, citron juice, orange juice, posca, lemon juice, and juice of unripe grapes. Since drinks of this sort cool and desiccate they do not quench thirst much but with their properties they repress putrefaction.

Bread prepared from flour with little bran and little salt, baked to perfection, is most favorable. It must be fresh but never hot, because as Hippocrates said, in *On Diet* and *On Regimen in Acute Diseases* 2, hot bread increases thirst and fills the body.[238] Averroes ordered, at the end of *Collectanea* 6, to abstain from all fatty, old, and thick meats.[239] I most greatly embrace this advice. Therefore, it will be beneficial to use the meat of birds, chickens, and veal, yet also care should be taken that these animals were nourished with the best feed. It will also be beneficial to cook at times unripe grape, sorrel, pimpinella,[240] borage, and bugloss with these meats. I also approved that the meat is cooked either in posca, rainwater, or rose water. Above all, it is best that these broths and meats are dressed with vinegar. It will be permitted sometimes, and especially in colder seasons, [86] to add aromatics, cinnamon, and cloves.

Fish should be renounced by virtually everyone as they favor the fomite of plague with their wetness. But in my opinion, not all should be renounced. I do not renounce at all fish that live near the shore or among rocks, because, if they are cooked to perfection and dressed, they greatly help, as they lower internal inflammation. They can be dressed with vinegar and pomegranate, lemon, orange, and barberry juice. Equally, soft, drinkable eggs dressed with *omphacium* and vinegar are approved.[241] I think there are no legumes that I could suggest for you. You know what Hippocrates thought about this, who said at the island Ainos many fell ill from eating legumes.[242] Therefore, I cannot approve of Averroes, who marvelously celebrated lentils, although I find this kind of food recommended also among other Arabs.[243]

All fruit, especially melons, must be avoided, as a corrupt juice is generated from them, which, as Galen said, even at the smallest opportunity causes malign fevers.[244] Fruit protected by wood-like shells and rinds can all be eaten without harm. For, Dioscorides said that pistachios are most greatly powerful against snake venom.[245] Avicenna says the same thing about almonds and hazelnuts.[246] You know how greatly famous is that antidote of Mithridates, king of Pontus, made out of nuts, figs, and leaves of rue.[247] Among the useful herbs are lemon balm, sorrel, borago, pimpinella, bugloss, sonchus, myrrh, endive; but rapeseed, mushrooms, tubers, radishes, leeks, and onions must be particularly avoided. There are those who think that in the time of pestilence the use of garlic is helpful, as Galen, in *Method of Healing* 12, called garlic the theriac of country folk.[248] But they are greatly mistaken since this kind of food produces inflamed humors, which above all greatly disturb body and soul with its foul odor. Thus, the poet Horace not incorrectly said "garlic more harmful than hemlock."[249] For all foods [87] the greatest care must be observed so that they are prepared to perfection, clean, without any filth, without any offensive appearance, and especially that they are taken from healthy locations.

## Chapter 23: What medications are useful for protection from the plague

In addition to diet for prevention, there are also certain beneficial medications, which are of two kinds. Some fortify the heart itself against poison, while others dilate and evacuate. Those that reinforce the heart against poison are either applied internally or externally. Those applied internally are Armenian bole, bezoar, unicorn horn powder, deer horn powder, red corral, and Cretan dittany—the dose of these powders is at most one dram. This powder is taken with wine, just as Galen gave Armenian bole with wine also for fevers. Moreover, there are various preparations, like Mithridates' preparation, theriac, citron preserve, sorrel preserve, and borago preserve. I usually use the preparation with this recipe:

> Sorrel preserve, 1 ounce
> Citron preserve, 1 ounce
> White Cretan dittany, 1 scruple
> Armenian bole, 1 scruple
> Zedoary, 1 scruple
> Mix.

Take half of an ounce or two or three drams of the preparation; afterward drink three or four ounces of broth of spring chicken, sorrel water, or light white wine.

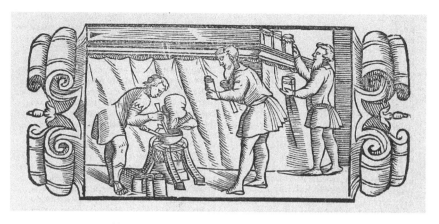

Figure 4. The preparation of compound medicines, from Giovanni
Da Vigo, *Prattica universale in cirurgia* (Venice: 1560), fol. 158r.
Courtesy of Countway Library, Harvard University Libraries.

Theriac should be smeared externally on the area around the heart with
lemon juice or rose vinegar. [88] Small sacks can also be applied, made from what
is in this recipe:

Orange flowers, 5 handfuls
Rose flowers, 5 handfuls
Borago flowers, 5 handfuls
All kinds of sandalwood, 3 drams
Agarwood, 3 drams
Camphor, 2½ drams
Saffron, 2½ drams
Gentian, 2½ drams
Aromatic reed, 2½ drams
White dittany, 2½ drams

All of these should be pulverized roughly and from these a small sack should
be made with purple silk cloth. I find that in our parents' time a similar kind
of extrinsic remedy was discovered, which they say even Pope Adrian VI used,
and it is that artificial orpiment called crystalline arsenic.[250] It has a double use.
One is that a raw piece of this arsenic should be worn beneath the area of the
heart; the other is that it is broken up and mixed with various powders, and a

paste is made, and this is dried into the shape of a large wheel and worn above the heart.

There are various ways of compounding, but I am most satisfied with this recipe:

Crystalline arsenic, 2 ounces
White dittany, 2 drams
Saffron, 2 drams
Camphor, 2 drams
Euphorbia, 1 dram

Reduce everything into a powder, and with as much rose water and gum arabic as necessary make a paste and let it dry out. [89] The faculty, by which this medication guards the heart from poison, can be secret and can be manifest. This orpiment, as Galen teaches, has a very caustic, drying faculty and dispels all putrefaction, just like fire, through its heat and dryness. In the same way we can think that arsenic, through its strong drying faculty, holds off every humor, whether putrid or liable to putrefaction, from the place of the heart.[251] But whatever it is, it is among those medications that experience teaches are beneficial.

Furthermore, medications that evacuate and dilate and are suitable for prevention are aloe and manna. For, all gums, Dioscorides said, are strong against poison, and our manna is a kind of gum; it drips off of trees like other gums or resins.[252] Syrup of rose solutive and syrup of polypody, these medications taken at intervals protect from plague. Among the aperients that are beneficial, there are all the cold seeds and roots of chicory, potentilla erecta, and sorrel. The times for using these medications is three or four hours before lunch, placed in spring chicken broth. Among the cures that evacuate, we can count cautery through which, as you know, watery discharges continually are expelled from the body. Cautery applied on the arms and shins is suitable for plague; it can also be done slightly below the groin. I found that cautery was recommended for preventing the plague by Niccolò the Florentine, a very important physician of his time.[253] But I will declare what I saw through my experience. I can testify that I saw countless people die from this plague and I never saw anyone who had undergone cautery [die], except for just one, and he was a priest. About this issue, I have also asked many physicians, who testified that they never saw anyone; therefore, it can be argued that this kind of assistance helps very much and with great reason, since through cautery [90] and through applying cloaca fluids that are either corrupt or liable to putrefaction are expelled.[254] And this is as much as must be said about the theory of prevention from plague.

## Chapter 24: On diet for pestiferous fevers

Now, it follows that we discuss treatment. This depends entirely on the removal of the disease and consequently of the symptoms. And since the diseases that are mostly spread in the plague are pestilential fevers, buboes, and carbuncles, I will discuss the cures of these, for, once these have been disposed, almost all symptoms that derive from them go away. Let me start with the treatment of pestiferous fevers: indications about cures for these are obtained from their nature. Since it is a hot intemperance with putrefying and poisoned matter, the goal of the physician must be to cool because of the intemperance. Its matter that is now putrefied indicates that it must be evacuated. Because of what is not yet putrefied but is putrefying, the goal must be to remove the putrefaction, which is done through what is called dilation and ventilation of the vessels. But since this matter, as I said, is poisoned, and the aforementioned poison is hostile to the heart through a secret power, from this another indication arises that the poison must be fought using those medications that protect the heart from it with a concealed faculty. For accomplishing this goal, there are three forms of treatment according to the ancients: regimen, pharmacy, and surgery.

As for what pertains to regimen, the entire theory that we showed must be observed for prevention should be engaged, namely, that the air should be improved and changed to cold and dry; sleep should be moderate; all motion of body and soul should be avoided; company should be avoided; [91] and the patients should always be held in the greatest peace; and if the stomach is constricted, it should be lightly softened. Common suppositories, although not sharp ones, are conducive for this softening. But in my opinion clysters are much more useful, especially those that are prepared out of material that is cooling and counteracts poisons. Rufus of Ephesus, according to Oribasius' *Medical Collections* 8.24, recommended clysters made out of only tepid water for malign fevers.[255] Rabbi Moses [Maimonides], in *Aphorisms* 10, approves clysters made of water and simple oil.[256] But I think clysters are much more effective that have something added to them that cools and counteracts poison in some way. A clyster prepared with this recipe is very effective:

Barley, 1 handful
Mallow leaves, ½ handful
Rose flowers, 1 handful
Citron rind, 1 handful

Boil together in common water according to standard practice.

Then, once it has been carefully strained, take:

1 pound of the above cooked liquid
½ pound of sweet almonds
2½ ounces of rose-honey solutive
Mix.

According to this formula you will be able prepare also others from chicken broth or other cooked liquids.

You must pay attention to what Rufus demanded: if the fever is great and burning, be careful that clysters should be administered that are so tepid that they are almost not felt at all.

About food and drink, there was great disagreement among physicians. For, some thought for pestiferous fevers a lot of food must be supplied; others, to the contrary, judged that the sick must eat little. Both are promoted by arguments and authorities. But because I have disputed this issue elsewhere and because this is not the time to expound on these debates, I shall say what my opinion is. Thus, I state that for these fevers, food must have wholesome juices and be easy to digest, such that the spirits that are continually drawn out can be easily and quickly regenerated. Furthermore, it is necessary to serve a small amount often; for, if only a small amount is offered, without doubt strength collapses. Indeed, Aëtius said, at 5.129, [92] based on the physician Herodotus' authority, that a lack of food increases the corruption of matter.[257] If, however, much food is served often, without doubt the strength sinks and, since the innate heat is weak, it can hardly digest, from which indigestions come to be and putrefaction grows from this undigested matter. Therefore, it is much more satisfactory, as I said, to present little food but often, like four or five times during the day and night. A useful food is crushed barley gruel made in spring chicken broth, to which pomegranate or citron juice is mixed in. Rose water is useful mixed in and also if barley is cooked in it. Bread in broth is helpful and useful; also gravies, in which there is unripe grape or barberry juice mixed in; and *panatella*[258] with citron juice.

I do not, however, approve of meats since they putrefy easily and since, in all fevers, as Hippocrates said, liquids are more useful than solid food. I greatly approve of a distillation made from meat that Avicenna calls "meat water" and, in *On the Powers of the Heart*, he writes that it is of the utmost help to the heart, especially if, while it is distilled, citron or lemon juice, leaves of borago, melissa, and rose vinegar are mixed in.[259] As for drink, barley water is suitable, or simple water boiled with pomegranate juice, vinegar, and barberry juice. I cannot recommend *jallab*, although I see it embraced by many books on practice.[260] The reason is because sweets of this kind often upset an otherwise badly affected stomach. Additionally, like all sweets, it readily increases internal inflammation. Therefore, I condemn everything sweet, pungent, and salty. Wine in no way should be allowed, in that it assails the head and increases intestinal burning. And do not let the authority of Galen, at *On Simple Medicines* 9, on the chapter on Samian earth, persuade you, when he uses wine for milder fevers and also greater ones, since he does not use it as nourishment but only as a vehicle for Armenian bole, which, since it is viscous [93] and cold, easily destroys all the damage that the wine can inflict.[261] In all foods for those suffering from pestilential fever one must be concerned that they have some power that repels poisons. Thus, it is appropriate to mix in powders of prepared pearls, red and white corals, deer horn, and bone from a deer's heart. You will also be able to approve of emerald powder, especially for princes, who can afford these luxuries. Another thing that must be watched out for in patients' foods is that no mistake is made, seeing that, if Hippocrates said, in *Epidemics* 1.2.19, that the daughter of that Philo lunched unhealthily and died, how much more must we fear other more serious mistakes that are often committed in diet?[262]

## Chapter 25: What medications help in curing pestilential fevers

The second way to treat pestiferous fevers is found in the use of pharmaceuticals. These are mainly two kinds: those that evacuate and those that strengthen. The strengthening kind are those that constrict the looseness of pores by cooling and drying and that restore and preserve the temperaments of organs, especially the heart. For, Galen said, in *On the Differences of Fevers* 5, that these organs are rendered weak because of the size of the pores and dyscrasia.[263] On the subject of evacuating medications, there was a quarrel among physicians about whether or not they ever help in the treatment of pestiferous fevers and about when they do help. There was no lack of those who thought that it is not appropriate to use evacuating medications but only those that strengthen and adjust.[264] Others, to the contrary, were of the opinion that evacuating is necessary; and this second group [94] was divided into two parts. Some sustained it should be purged immediately, others not unless the matter had been prepared. The reason for this controversy was nothing other than that this impurity of pestiferous fevers is such that, as Jacques [Despars] said, no matter what, most often the death of the patient follows.[265] For, whether we abstain from pharmaceuticals or we use them, and we use them either right away or later, the entire situation is full of danger. And, as I said, most patients die.

But in order that I do not detain you at this time with doubtful questions, above all, I establish four conclusions in this matter. One is that pestiferous fevers arise from a significant putrefaction. This putrefaction often arises suddenly. The second is that putrid and poisoned matter must be removed as soon as possible from the body, in that, since it can neither be improved nor take on a benign nature, out of necessity, it contaminates and corrupts whatever it touches. The third is that, in pestiferous fevers, the natural powers are dislodged as quickly as possible for no reason other than that this matter's poison destroys the whole temperament of the heart. A weakness of the faculty happens, as I said based on Galen's opinion, from dyscrasia. The fourth and final one is that the matter of putrid fevers, as it is putrid, requires the kind of pharmaceuticals that purge; but, as it is poisonous and utterly annihilating, a specific remedy is required that can be discovered only through experience.

Consequently, during the plague in the time of Rufus of Ephesus, the suitable treatment was a compound made from myrrh, aloe, and saffron, that Rufus himself invented.[266] Thus, also in the time Emperor Marcus Aurelius waged war in Parthia, a plague developed in which he cured all of the sick with oil and wine, as Arrian and Simplicius, in the *Categories*, write.[267] Elsewhere I said the same thing about human urine, Armenian bole, and theriac, with whose assistance, Galen recorded, various plagues were cured. And we have no reason to think that Armenian bole and theriac [95] are beneficial in cases of plague only by a faculty of drying, since there are many medications that dry more strongly and yet it is not confirmed by experience that they are beneficial. But, indeed, if we should penetrate Galen's mind, at *On Simple Medicines* 9, after he listed the effects that Armenian bole creates by drying, he adds another effect, as if he had sustained there to be some other power in it that counteracts plague besides desiccation, just like he also did in *On Theriac for Piso* 16, where after he praised the divine Hippocrates, who cured plague not simply with fire but with a fire made from aromatics, said that he made theriac that was just like this fire, not simple but purgative, that is, which, in addition to a desiccating power, had some other faculty that, I say, wards off plague itself.[268] Thus, it is established among all that, besides the desiccating power, which, as Avicenna said, can be achieved through phlebotomy and purging, some other secret faculty is required that can resist this poison.[269]

With these conclusions established, I assert that in every pestiferous fever, unless something prevents it, there must be evacuation and purging right away. For, if incontestably swelling matter, as Hippocrates reminds, must be expelled from the body as soon as possible, in that there is danger that it attacks a noble organ, then so much the more must we immediately evacuate and purge when the poisoned matter has seized the heart, the very seat of life. Therefore, there must be an evacuation very quickly, since, as Hippocrates says, if something must be changed, change at the start.[270]

There are many purgatory medications suitable for these fevers, some that are found in a solid form, others that are liquid. Among those that are found in a solid form, there is soothing electuary and rose electuary. Many also approve of the so-called "benedicta" compound,[271] taken in the quantity of three drams with four ounces of water of endive. [96] Among the solids, we can also count colocynth pills, which Averroes, at *Collectanea* 7.31, greatly recommends for the treatment of pestiferous carbuncles.[272] And euphorbia is recommended by many for this problem, and this is the way the recipe should be prepared:

Euphorbia, 12 grains
Mastic, 8 grains
White dittany, 4 grains
Make a ball with honey in rose solutive.

Among the ancients, I find that Avenzoar most greatly recommended euphorbia; many later physicians then followed his opinion.[273] Many also praise tamarinds and correctly. If you would like to use them in the summer, use this recipe:

Pulp of tamarinds, 6 drams
Mesue's rose electuary, 2½ drams
Mix.

This is a very suitable medication.

If you would like to give some medication as a drink, you have senna, dodder,[274] and agaricus,[275] which Avicenna counts among the cordial medications.[276]
You can prepare this medication with the following recipe:

Dodder leaves, 1½ drams
Senna, 1½ drams
Violet flowers, ½ bunch
Borago flowers, ½ bunch
Water Germander, 1½ drams
Citron seeds, 1½ drams
Make a decoction according to standard practice.

Then take:
The above decoction, 4 ounces
Prepared agaricus, 4 scruples
Choice rhubarb, 3½ scruples
Spike lavender, 3 grains
Camphor, 3 grains
Pour out all of these according to the standard practice. Then, after it
     has been carefully strained, add 3½ ounces of syrup of rose solutive.
     Mix. We can use manna in place of the syrup of rose solutive.

And pay attention that in compounding these medications, the poison must
always be kept in mind: something always should be mixed in that protects the
heart from poison.

     Among the resolvents, we can also count the cold, which is greatly approved
for treating these kinds of fevers by Avicenna. And we experienced last year that
this kind of medication helped many cases as they were burning fevers for the most
part, as you heard. Besides evacuation that comes from resolvent medications,
evacuation through sweating is also usually useful, in that, when stimulated in this
way it expels through sweat just as it is accustomed to [97] expel spontaneously
when it is excited naturally. Barley water is greatly recommended for these cases; if
it is consumed in a great quantity, then it overwhelms the body itself. Also, barley
water with sedge can be prepared; one and half drams of powder of *leucojum* or
violets taken before drinking the barley water can marvelously provoke sweat.

     After a purge, and even if a purge cannot be done, we must go down to those
medications that adjust and strengthen the vital organs. Avicenna greatly recommends the use of goat whey for altering intrinsically.[277] Thus, also spring chicken

broth, sprinkled with cordial herbs, like melissa, pimpinella, sorrel, cicely, helps most greatly and usually significantly alters corrupt humors.

Also, confections can be made. And, because we said that in summer all sweets must be avoided, you could compound the pieces with this recipe.

> Armenian bole, 1 scruple
> Burnt deer horn, 1 scruple
> Red corral, 1 scruple
> Gentian, 1 scruple
> Make a ball with lemon or citron juice.

But if it is winter, it will be also permitted to mix either chicory or sorrel preserves in the powders.

Of those medicines that must be applied to the heart in this period, I find it debated whether it is better to administer cooling and astringent medications or rather heating and drying ones. I like more those medications that are compounded from what cools, without restricting, and dries and can moderately assist the heart. This compress is made from this recipe:

> Rose water, 1 pound
> Melissa, 1 pound
> Sorrel, 1 pound
> Camphor, ½ scruple
> Saffron, ½ scruple
> Citron rinds, 1½ handfuls
> Germander, 1½ ounces
> White dittany, 1½ ounces
> Boil together, and then make a compress according to the usual custom with either a linen or silk cloth.

Besides this compress, also a liniment is suitable with this recipe:

> The best theriac, 1 dram
> Powder of all kinds of sandalwood, 1½ scruples
> Germander, 1½ scruples
> White dittany, 1½ scruples
> A little bit of lemon juice
> Mix, and make the liniment.

## [98] Chapter 26: On surgical assistance
## that should be used for pestiferous fevers

I speak of treatments that can be used for fighting these pestilential fevers, as the third and final way of treating is achieved through surgical operations. Since there are multiple kinds, first, we must look at drawing blood. There is the oldest quarrel about whether or not blood should be drawn for pestiferous fevers. Many denied that it should be drawn. There is no lack of those who affirmed that it should be drawn; and these were divided, since some approved more of phlebotomy, others cupping, and others leeches. The cause of this disagreement, just as I said for medications, was that most of the patients die no matter what a physician does, not from the incorrectness of the remedy but rather from the strength and corruption of the disease itself. Therefore, since I have disputed this question most fully elsewhere, now I shall only briefly say what you must settle on. Therefore, two conclusions must be established for you. First, only when the bodily powers are present at the beginning of pestiferous fevers should the blood always be drawn. I said only when the bodily powers are at hand because also at the start the powers were usually completely expelled by the poison.

I approve of drawing blood because, above all, Avicenna's authority confirmed it, when he said the cure of pestiferous diseases depends on desiccation; he added that this can be done through pharmaceuticals and by drawing blood.[278] Also theory confirms it because, if incontestably the poison must be removed most quickly from the body and the poison itself rests in the putrefying blood, clearly, if the blood is carried off, then the foundation and fomite of the poison are carried off. Nothing hinders the matter from being corrupt and, therefore, to need the relaxing of the stomach more than the drawing of blood, because Galen, at *Method of Healing* 4.6, where he stated that blood must always be drawn for great diseases, declaring [99] what the great diseases are, said they are called great either from the degree of suffering, the importance of the organ, or *dia tēn kakoēthian*, that is, because of corruption, as he had clearly taught that blood should also be drawn for corrupt and malign diseases.[279]

However, there are two rules that must be carefully observed if possible. One is that the theory of repletion should be considered, which not only Galen but also Avicenna, Paul, and Aëtius seem to require in these cases.[280] And this is according to theory, because, if the repletion is slight, the most sparing amount of blood must be drawn, given that the poison cannot be very lethal. If it is a

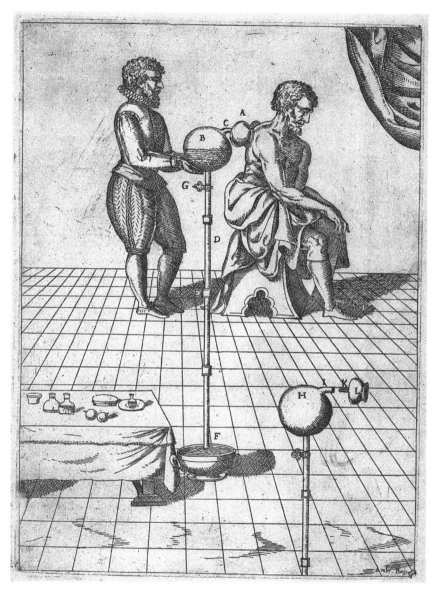

Figure 5. An etching of a surgeon using cupping tools to extract blood, made by Ambrogio Brambilla, who was active in Rome from 1579 to 1599. Courtesy of the Wellcome Collections (https://creativecommons.org/licenses/by/4.0/).

little greater, the drawing of blood also must be more copious. If it is significant, the greatest drawing of blood must be done. And for this reason, those physicians who think blood must be drawn in these cases until fainting do not deceive you, because they look at the greatest repletion, which usually is connected with pestiferous fever. The other rule that must be heeded is that, in the hottest constitutions, if it is possible, you should draw no blood or very little. Indeed, Galen's opinion, at *On [Regimen in] Acute Diseases* 4.19, was that at the height of summer blood should not be drawn, even if the disease is great and the natural powers allow for it.[281] In fact, at the beginning of *For Glaucon* 14, he said that physicians often seriously err who draw blood in the hotter seasons and adds that in that constitution almost everyone whose blood was drawn died.[282]

The second conclusion that we must establish is that the drawing of blood should never be considered, unless you are summoned at the beginning. I am led to affirm this by Galen's authority, at *Commentary on Epidemics* 1.3.26, when, asking why Hippocrates in the case of Criton did not mention venesection, he says the reason was because Hippocrates was not summoned at the beginning, as if he wished to teach us that if Hippocrates had been summoned at the beginning, he would have opened the vein, despite there being a great impurity present. [100] Because of this impurity, black pustules appeared immediately on the miserable patient and he died on the third day.[283] Therefore, when it will be permitted to draw blood, venesection must always be chosen such that, if sickness appears in the higher parts of the body, the blood should be drawn from the basilic vein. If, however, the sickness is propagated into the lower parts, in the groin, hips, or below the liver, the popliteal vein should be chosen, so that just as it tries to discharge itself naturally into these parts, you help it in the same way.

However, if it is not permitted to open the vein, because of age or for some other reason, we have cupping tools and leeches. Blood can be extracted by leeches applied either to hemorrhoids or also to the feet, in accordance with what the attack of disease will appear to demand. We can also employ cupping tools. Physicians disagreed not a little about the place where they should be put. I prefer that the cupping tools are placed below the liver, above the buttocks, and below the buttocks, in that, since these instruments powerfully attract, it is much more successful if they attract the poison to parts that are far from the heart rather than close to it.

If patients can endure scarifications and our assistants know this kind of procedure, without doubt, I would also like this kind of assistance that is found greatly praised in Galen and in Oribasius based on Apollonius' opinion.[284] But just as I have argued at great length elsewhere, this kind of procedure is not in use.

I say that it is not in use since, in my opinion, scarifications, scarring cupping, and light cupping differ greatly according to medical writers. But there is no reason to speak longer about this since, as I said, it has been carefully discussed by us.

Among surgical procedures we can count that kind of remedy that is called vesicatory. These vesicatory procedures draw the poison from the heart to less noble parts, whether the poison is in vapors or in humors. [101] Do not believe it is a new kind of remedy without any theory. It is extremely ancient, as you could see in Galen, at *On Medicines by Part* 6.1, for there, based on Archigenes' opinion of those who are tormented from winds distending the stomach, he greatly approves that we place a sponge soaked in the most pungent vinegar on the arms and legs until pustules arise.[285] Also, Oribasius, in *Medical Collections* 8.19, lists pungent medications applied to joints, among the remedies that best send away poison and corrupt humors from the noble organs.[286] Likewise, Galen, at *On Humors* 1, writes, just as also Rabbi Moses [Maimonides] says, in *Aphorisms*, that when a humor is brought to the head or the stomach, stinging medicines applied to the hands and feet greatly help.[287] Jacques Despars, who lived more than two hundred years ago, made the clearest reference to our vesicatories. Indeed, he described almost the same shape and material that we use. Indeed, in his commentary on [*Canon*] 4.1, in the chapter on pestilential fever, among the remedies that he writes that help, he lists vesicatories applied to the arms and legs, made of milk, fig, euphorbia, or blister beetles with yeast, so it must not be doubted that this kind of protection is old.[288] The place, therefore, where these remedies are to be applied is on the arms, three inches above the wrist and on the front of the shin a little above the malleolus bones. There are different substances that we use for making vesicatories. But sometimes we employ clematis and that herb called "deer's foot."[289] For, this herb is crushed and applied sometimes by itself, sometimes soaked in the most pungent vinegar. But, as I said, most frequently of all we use blister beetles together with yeast. I greatly approve of blister beetles, in that, Hippocrates and Dioscorides reported that they are greatly effective against poison.[290] Therefore, you will be able to prepare a vesicatory with this recipe: [102]

> Prepared blister beetles, 3 drams
> Yeast, 1½ ounces
> Mix with a small amount of the most pungent vinegar and make a
>     paste.

Either mustard or euphorbia can sometimes be added, just as I taught (if I am not wrong) at great length in the treatise on compounding medicines.[291] The shape of the vesicatory must be either round, or oval, more or less three inches in length and breadth. It should be used such that at any time, both before or after lunch, it is placed on the aforementioned places before being heated either through rubbing or a hot lotion. When this remedy is positioned, it should be held there until it provokes blisters, which usually happens sometimes in ten hours, sometimes in twenty, sometimes more, sometimes less. When the blisters are produced, they break so that fluid flows out, and where they have broken, butter with a cabbage leaf should be placed on them and kept on for one or two days. Then, in place of the butter, holy unguent should be placed on the ulcerated body part. But, if it provokes pain, the holy unguent should be removed, and in its place either a rose unguent or simple liniment should be rubbed in to placate the pain. Once the pain has subsided, again apply the holy unguent, by which, as long as it remains, the wounds should be kept open until the sickness is absolutely finished. And unless it solidifies by itself, that plaster called "diapalma" should be applied in order to induce a scar. [292] So much for these pestilential fevers.

## Chapter 27: On pestilential buboes

Among all the disorders that are often seen in the plague, frequently tumors are accustomed to appear, which arise on various and different parts, below the ears, under the armpits, and on the groins, and sometimes are bigger, sometimes smaller, sometimes minute, sometimes with pain, sometimes without. All these tumors, however, are called by the common [103] name from the Greek, buboes; this name today is also used in Latin. And the reason for this name is that those[293] glands, in which they arise, are called buboes by Hippocrates and other physicians, as you have the testimony in Galen in many places but especially in the commentary on *Epidemics* 2; you will find a fragment of these commentaries that I translated into Latin that was very recently printed by Giunta.[294] There is a difference among these tumors, in that, most frequently they arise in the groin and for this reason the plague is called inguinal; more rarely they are found under the armpits; and most rarely of all they come to be below the ears.

There is a most powerful explanation for why in almost all plagues these kinds of tumors are seen: the pestiferous poison is so hostile to [the body's] nature, that not only is it disturbed in guarding the organs from it, but also it tries to expel it from all parts of the body. And since the glands are the weakest of all body parts, for this reason, the poison, having been pushed into these parts, frequently produces tumors. I said that the [body's] nature expels this poison also from other parts, in that, there is a double generation of these pestiferous buboes. The first and the strongest is when the heart is directly affected by the poison and its agitated power expels it. The second mode of generation is when the heart is not affected directly but, through contagion or for some other reason, one or another part of the body having been contaminated pushes the poison that it has within itself into a weaker part. There is a difference in these modes of generation because when the tumors arise from the heart having been directly attacked, most usually a fever precedes or at least accompanies [the tumors]; when they come to be from a heart that is not directly attacked, a fever does not accompany them continually, but they come to be at the start without a fever and indeed sometimes persist without any fever. The true reason why they arise more frequently on the groin and very rarely on the head is that this matter [104] is thick, sticky, and viscous and consequently more easily carried downward when expelled by [the body's] nature; but the groins, since they are below the infected parts, most readily of all assume this matter that is otherwise descending through its own force. However, even if the head, as Hippocrates said, at *On Diseases* 4, because of its size and hollowness, easily receives humors and diseases, nevertheless, these pestiferous humors, because of their viscosity and stickiness, are not easily drawn into the head, and are not easily lifted upward, but only the vapors, having risen to the head, bring about other symptoms, which you have heard.[295] And it should not worry you that this pestiferous matter, from which papules arise, attacks the face and head most of all because this matter is dispersed throughout the whole body and because, when it is moved by a great force, it is brought into the face and head, which readily receive it. It is different for the matter of pestiferous fevers and for the matter of buboes, which does not rise easily from there into the upper parts of the head, since it is not dispersed throughout the whole body but hides in the interior parts of the body.

A pestiferous tumor is easily diagnosed both because of the plague passing through and because of the severe characteristics that accompany it, for, there is deliria, dementia, vomiting, unclear urine, and many other severe symptoms, which make it easy to distinguish a pestilential tumor from a non-pestilential one. Because, even if non-pestilential buboes come to be during the plague, as was ascertained in our era, nevertheless, as they are not pestiferous, they do not have fevers, except ones that last one day, as Hippocrates and Galen teach in the *Aphorisms*; and they do not have dementia, vomiting, and corrupt urine, like the pestiferous ones have.[296] Every pestilential bubo is lethal; and the more hidden and smaller it is, the worse it usually is, so that patients with them die on the second, third, and fourth days.

I said that sometimes there are buboes without fevers. It is debated whether a bubo or any other [105] pestiferous disorder can arise without fever. On the one hand, it seems that it can arise, first on the authority of Hippocrates, at *Epidemics* 3.3, text 60, where, after he recounted many kinds of diseases, he says that none of those sick with fever were disobedient.[297] From this passage you can infer that some sick with plague were without fever. Also, at text 55 from the same book and often elsewhere, he names many and even dangerous symptoms, of which he says some are with fever and others without fever.[298] Galen, also, in the chapter on Armenian bole in *On Simple Medicines* 9, writes that in the plague that medication was delivered with wine to some who were without fever but to others without wine.[299] Hence, it is quite obvious that the plague attacked some without fever. Our testimony also supports this, since in this plague, carbuncles and buboes were seen without fever.

On the other hand, there are authorities and arguments that convince that no pestiferous diseases can be without fever. And there is the preeminent authority of Hippocrates himself in *On Breaths*, where, dividing fevers into common and particular, he says that common fevers are plague, as he wanted fever to be completely inseparable from plague.[300] Paul, Aëtius, Avicenna, Rhazes, and almost all others, when they discussed plague, you will observe that they discussed it among pestilential fevers.[301] Indeed, it can be argued that, according to their opinion, fever is almost essential to the plague itself and all pestiferous disease. But, in addition to authorities, theory is not lacking. For, plague, without doubt, is an acute disease, in fact, the most acute. Because given that the character of an acute disease is fast movement with danger, as Archigenes said, [and] without doubt the plague moves fast because it kills quickly and it is dangerous, in that it kills the majority of those sick with it, therefore, it is also with fever.[302] This conclusion is approved by Hippocrates' and Galen's authority. For, Hippocrates writes, at *Epidemics* 1.3.3, [106] that the most acute and most difficult diseases are conjoined with continual fever.[303] Galen also, in *Aphorisms* 1.7 and near the end of *On Difficulty in Breathing* 3, writes that fevers are inseparable from acute disease.[304] A second argument supports this, because, if plague, as Galen put forward, at *On the Differences of Fevers* 1.4, is generated from a putrefaction inflamed around the heart, in no way can it happen that this occurs without fever, that is, that a significant putrefaction arises in the heart without heat first being inflamed and then expanded through the whole body.[305]

For the resolution of this question, it must be established for you that buboes and pestiferous carbuncles never can come to be without fever; non-pestiferous tumors and carbuncles, however, can come to be without fever, even when they arise during the time of a pestilence. But what should we say to the relevant authorities? We can respond in two ways. First, a fever either is significant, slight, or barely apparent. Plague, indeed, can sometimes arise and be without a significant fever, just as Galen teaches, in *On Simple Medicines* 9.[306] But the plague can never be without fever, even if sometimes slight and barely sensible. And therefore, when Hippocrates tells that some of the sick were without fever, it must be understood as significant fever. The second way we can respond is that fever can either precede, follow, or accompany the plague. If we should speak about fever that can precede buboes or another pestiferous disease, without doubt it is not necessary that a fever of this kind that precedes other pestiferous diseases is continually connected to plague, because, as you have learned, the bubo and carbuncles come to be not only when the heart has been directly struck but also other body parts. But, if we should speak about fevers that can accompany and follow close after pestiferous disorders, I say that it cannot happen that any pestiferous disorder is found that does not have some fever, either accompanying or subsequent. You can infer this solution from the great Hippocrates, at *Epidemics* [107] 3.3.28, where it is most clearly concluded that fever sometimes follows pestiferous diseases, sometimes accompanies, and sometimes also precedes.[307] In our pestilence, carbuncles and buboes, however, were seen without fever; this happened because these were not pestiferous. And it is also not incongruous, as I said, that in the time of plague, tumors and other non-pestiferous disorders come to be, just as non-pestilential fevers and other diseases arise. Or, if they were pestiferous, they had some subsequent, preceding, and accompanying fevers, but slight and gentle. It is certain that in the time of pestilence many of these come to be.

## Chapter 28: Treatment of bubonic pestilence

The treatment of pestiferous buboes, which pertains to pharmacy, diet, and surgical operations, is nearly the same as what we described for pestilential fevers. As a result, I would think it superfluous to repeat the same diet, the same pharmaceuticals, and the same surgical assistance. Thus, only the treatment that uses topical cures specifically for buboes must be discussed. And we should find appropriate help, if we hold before our eyes the goals needed for this sickness. The bubo is a preternatural tumor. Thus, since the tumor's great mass is combined with inflammation, it indicates to us that its great mass must be removed and the inflammation repressed. Therefore, for the sake of its inflammation, cooling medications must be used. For the sake of its size, which happens because of the growth of matter, it is indicated that this matter must be removed and withdrawn. But because this matter harms not only with its size but also with its contaminated and poisoned quality, attention must be paid to two things here. First, [108] that this matter is completely extracted and that it is done most rapidly in order that, remaining, it does not diffuse the poison far and wide. The second is that, since it is in a non-noble body part, we do not expel the poison into the interior of the body with cooling medications that otherwise are appropriate for the inflammation.

For this reason, the chief goal must be drawing out and evacuating as quickly as possible. This evacuation can happen either perceptibly or imperceptibly. There are many aids for drawing out and evacuating imperceptibly. First of all, there is the dry and fiery cupping tools, which once applied draws out and even imperceptibly dissipates. There is also the unguent called "diachylon."[308] Some also apply dove or chicken; for, they cut off the rear parts of these animals while still living and they apply them while still warm, then the poison is drawn by the heat from these parts and dispersed. Applications of dove manure perform the same thing. The drawing out and evacuation is done also perceptibly so that the scarring cupping tool is placed on the body part or one nearby; leeches can be applied as well, or a lancet. Also, a vesicatory and cautery are to be applied right away so that this poisoned matter is drawn out and consumed at the same time; these should be done right at the first stage of the appearance of pestiferous tumors. When enough matter has been drawn out so there is no chance that the poison returns inside, all attention must be directed toward the ripening of its drawn-out matter, which is done with plasters and unguents. The unguent called "great diachylon" is greatly recommended, also plasters that are made from mallow, the roots of hibiscus, onions, saffron, and terebinth. And so you have a few versions, the first will be this plaster with this recipe:

Fresh butter, 1 ounce
Pig fat, 1 ounce
Terebinth, 1½ ounces
Saffron, ½ scruple
Water germander, ½ scruple
Mix and make a plaster.

Another version is for a stronger plaster, with this recipe:

> Hibiscus root, cooked and passed through a sieve, 1½ ounces [109]
> Lily bulb, ½ ounce
> Dittany, 1½ dram
> Water germander, 1½ dram
> Mix and make a plaster.

These plasters must be removed often, at least three times day and night, in that, since the tumor's poison is drawn off by the plaster, the more it is changed, the better is the drawing off.

When the tumor has ripened, it must be opened right away. And take note that pestiferous tumors must be opened before all arrive at ripeness, since, as I said, this poison must be removed as quickly as it can be done. The method for opening is with a lancet or with corrosive and caustic medications; these are the sort compounded out of soap and quicklime. When the tumor is opened, the wound must be most carefully cleaned; terebinth with honey and germander is most preferred for doing this. I often add germander, as no other assistance is better than it for this poisoned putrefaction. But, if it should happen that this diseased flesh grows over this ulcer, it must be covered either with powder of calcined alum or what is called Egyptian unguent.[309] Once the wound has been cleaned, next, the flesh should be regrown; this is done by those powders called sarcotic. Here is a recipe for them:

> Resin of sarcocolla,[310] 2 drams
> Burnt olive leaves, 2 drams
> Frankincense, 2 drams
> Water germander, 2 drams
> Iris roots, ½ dram
> Mix. Spread these powders over the wound, and then apply ceruse
>     unguent or something similar over the powders.

When the flesh has regrown and the whole wound has filled up, it remains to induce scarring. This it done either with a wax plaster called "diapalma" or that unguent of white camphor. And I praise this white camphor unguent because of the camphor, which is greatly potent against poisons and pestiferous matter.

## [110] Chapter 29: On pestilential carbuncles

Among the disorders, there is also that one most common to the plague that is called by the Greeks *anthrax*, and in Latin "carbo" or "carbunculus."[311] The barbarians, who often are unskilled with names, distinguished between carbuncle and anthrax but, among the best writers on medicine, anthrax is that same thing as carbuncle. There are two kinds of carbuncles: one non-pestilential, the other indeed pestilential. Pliny spoke about the non-pestilential one, at [*Natural History*] 26.1, where he writes that a carbuncle peculiar to the province of Narbonne first came to Italy during the censorship of Lucius Paullus and Quintus Marcius.[312]

The pestilential carbuncle, however, that pertains to what we are speaking is either an ulcerated tumor or not ulcerated; this tumor comes to be from a thick, burnt, putrefying, and poisoned humor. It hardens because of the thickness of the humor; from the burning it has a red color in its base; a little above the base it is black and at the apex it has a white blister. The reason why it has these various colors is because, since the humor is inflamed and burning, like the nature of fiery things, the fire and flame always seek the upper parts. Hence it comes to be so that it is red at the base; above the base, where there is more fire, it blackens; and at the apex, where the greatest burning comes to be, there is a blister. As a consequence of all these, there is great pain and agony. Because of the putrefaction, the carbuncle is rendered foul-smelling, as Hippocrates, at *Epidemics* 3, deservedly had called carbuncles *sēpseis*, that is putrefactions, of the truest kind.[313] Because of the poison, the carbuncle is rendered so contagious that the tumor is inflamed, painful, foul-smelling, and contagious. For this reason, when the blister is broken, not only the tumor but also the wound is pestiferous and foul-smelling. Because of its similarity to coal, the writers on agriculture called carbuncle and [111] carbunculation a kind of disorder of trees and vines, when the tips of buds of the trees are burnt by the cold and rot, and also when the vines, having shed their leaves under the burning sun, dry up and the juices flow out.

Just like a tumor, the carbuncle has two ways of being generated. First, when the heart, directly affected, expels the poison away from itself toward the extremities; the second, when the other body parts, contaminated either by contagion or by air, generate poison in themselves and, once thus generated, they thrust it into the non-noble parts. Fever always either precedes or accompanies the first carbuncles; it is not necessary that a fever precedes but that, at least, it follows those last ones. It does not escape me that carbuncles also come to be without fever, as I said, but those ones are not pestilential whenever a fever does not precede or at least does not follow or accompany. Since Nicephorus

Callistus, at [*Ecclesiastical History*] 7.28, and Eusebius, at [*Ecclesiastical History*] 9.6, write that, during the rule of Emperor Maximinus, the plague attacked with the sore that is called anthrax and, creeping through the whole body and attacking the eyes, blinded almost everyone; that sore, in my opinion, was not truly a carbuncle but rather wasting sores of that kind that developed in the Athenian plague that Thucydides narrates.[314] And I also think this disorder was similar to what Galen recounts at *On Venesection* 7, where he writes that some putrefying wounds sometimes exposed the place below the bordering skin, that is, its base, so that the veins appeared uncovered; and he says the same things continually appeared on the whole body when a certain foul pox of carbuncles attacked the Asian populations.[315] And take note so that the Latin translator of Eusebius does not deceive you, since, he says that this kind of carbuncle was new and foreign, but the Greek text does not have this in anyway, and neither does Nicephorus, who took everything from Eusebius, nor Rufinus, the old translator of Eusebius.[316] And also, [112] it cannot be true, since, if, as we said that carbuncles are a common disorder of the plague, how can it have happened that it is a new and foreign sickness?

You will recognize the carbuncles because they have those colors that I have described and pain, and, besides these, they have other associated severe symptoms, like sleeplessness, thirst, intestinal burning, deliria, drowsiness, and fiery and unclear urine. Nearly every pestilential carbuncle is lethal; and the smaller it is, as I also said elsewhere, the worse it is; accordingly, the greater and wider they are, the more they promise a return to health.

## Chapter 30: On the treatment of pestilential carbuncles

The theory for the treatment of carbuncles with respect to regimen, the use of pharmaceuticals, and surgical intervention is the same as what we laid out for pestiferous fever. The one difference can be that when the carbuncles appear, the medications to be delivered must be stronger, like the scammony mixture praised by Averroes, because, if this otherwise thick, burnt humor is to be extracted, it needs the strongest remedy.[317] There must also be a more copious drawing of blood when carbuncles are present than when simple tumors are present, since the burning and heat is the greatest of all with the carbuncles. As a result, the opportune application of cold is more favored for these than for tumors or other pestiferous disorders. Proper and necessary local treatment of carbuncles must be chosen completely in accordance with its nature. For, a tumor is made out of a burning, putrefying, and poisoned humor. Because of this, as we said about tumors, the physician's foremost goal must be that the matter is evacuated from that part. This can happen in various and different ways. First, the removal of this matter is done with a lancet, for, as soon as that blister appears it is best [113] to incise it, so that its venom is breathed out.[318] And there was advice of this kind in Galen's *Method of Healing* 14 and Avicenna. If it cannot be done with a lancet, either because of the patient's fear or some other impediment, a caustic or vesicatory should be applied immediately so that the poison flows out from the opened tumor. The physician has three goals before him, after having opened the carbuncle. First, that the putrefying matter dries out; second, that the burning and heat is lessened; and third, that the matter's poison is stifled. Therefore, physicians usually compound medications that regard these three goals, like that which is made from plantain juice, germander, lentils, and bran bread. This recipe is an example of this:

Boiled lentils, 1½ ounces
Bran bread, 1½ ounces
Oak gall powder, 1½ drams
Water germander, 1½ drams
Plantain juice, 1 ounce
Mix. Make a plaster that must be changed often during the day and
    night, since it becomes poisoned itself if it remains for too long on
    the carbuncles, and similarly, if it is changed often, it more effec-
    tively attracts the poison into itself and it cools and dries.

Often an intolerable agony is regularly connected to carbuncles. In this case, milk with bran bread and plantain juice helps marvelously in placating the pain. It should be goat milk or cow milk. But if the carbuncle is very malignant and danger is imminent, two things must be done in order that the ulcer does not creep into nearby parts and destroys them. First, the nearby parts are to be protected with cooling and drying medications, that is, with plantain juice, lentils cooked in vinegar, Armenian bole, vinegar, egg whites, and snake's blood. For, by having these nearby parts anointed, the danger of their corruption is easily avoided. The second is that medicines that can powerfully dry, such as caustics, are to be applied to these ulcerated parts. And above all in these cases what is most useful and praised by Galen are Andron's lozenge,[319] Egyptian unguent, and [114] Apostles' unguent.[320] Also, vinegar with a little alum and verdigris is a most powerful desiccant and can repress the carbuncle's putrefaction. Also, for these medications what I warned must be obeyed, that they are changed often. But if these medications do not help at all, fire must be used and the carbuncles burned off, for, neither medications nor the blade can do what fire does, as Hippocrates said.[321] After the carbuncle's crust has fallen off and what is popularly called the root is extracted, it remains that the wound is carefully cleaned. To do this, honey and hot oak charcoal works very well; Pliny, at the end of book 36 [of the *Natural History*], writes that this charcoal finishes off pestiferous carbuncles.[322] Also, the unguent made from honey and sarcocolla, described by Rhazes, in *For Almansor* 7, works for the same purpose.[323] Also, terebinth, which, as I said, helps by its property, together with egg yolk and honey, works wonderfully. Once the wound has been evacuated and cleaned, the [regrowth of] flesh and scarring must be induced. And, if some excess flesh grows, it must be shaved off in the same way and with the same remedies that I demonstrated for buboes. And this is the end of my discussion on pestilence, which I promised you. May it please immortal God to turn this disaster away from us and save us, so that we can work for you and follow our lessons during the time of Lent.

# GLOSSARY

*Andron's lozenge.* A compound medicine that typically contained gall, myrrh, alum, pomegranate seeds, vinegar, and wine.

*anthrax.* The Greek name for a carbuncle.

*aperient.* A medication that opens up the body's pores either internally or externally.

*Apostles' unguent.* A compound medicine that typically contained alum, myrrh, mastic, rose oil, and terebinth.

*Armenian bole.* A yellowish, friable, earthy clay containing aluminum silicates and iron oxide that frequently was used in ancient, medieval, and early modern pharmacology for its astringent qualities.

*attraction.* A natural faculty or power of the body and its organs that plays an important role in physiological processes like digestion and nutrition by moving matter within the body.

*Auster.* The southerly wind that often brings hot and humid air associated with plagues.

*basilic vein.* A large superficial vein in the arm.

*bilious humors.* Humors or bodily fluids in which bile predominates. Bile was categorized as either red or yellow bile, with a hot and dry temperament, or as black bile, in which case, it is characterized by coldness and dryness.

*bubo.* The swelling of a lymph node characteristic of bubonic plague. Buboes typically developed in the groin and armpits and on the neck.

*cantharides.* A beetle from the family Meloidae that secretes catharidin, a blistering agent that is poisonous in larger doses. Dried and ground up, it was used as an ingredient for vesicatories. It is also called blister beetle or Spanish Fly.

*carbuncle.* A large boil or group of boils on the skin. Its name comes from the Latin word for a small piece of coal because of the wound's red base and white apex, which are similar in appearance to a burning coal. Mercuriale identified the term carbuncle with the Greek term *anthrax.*

*cautery.* The application of a heated metallic instrument to sear bodily tissue or change the flow of humors within the body.

*clyster.* The injection of curative or soothing liquids through the rectum. It is also referred to as an enema.

*common disease.* An illness that is widespread in a population or in several populations.

*compound.* A medicine that is made of multiple ingredients mixed together.

*concoction.* The process of transforming substances through heat. A concept used to explain diverse physiological and biological processes including digestion and ripening. The word was also used to explain artificial transformations using heat, such as those that occur in culinary practices.

*confection.* Medicine made in the form of small balls similar to pieces of candy.

*constitution.* The general circumstances of a given place, with particular emphasis on meteorological conditions and the "constitution of the air." The term also refers to a particular case history of an epidemic that includes a description of its underlying causes and development. It is a translation of the Greek word *katastasis*, which is used in the Hippocratic corpus.

*contagion.* The transmission of a disease from one body to another. The term usually refers to transmission either through direct contact or fomites. But Mercuriale also considered transmission through air to be a kind of contagion.

*cupping.* The application of a heated glass cup to the body to extract blood.

*decoction.* Liquid extracted from substances, typically parts of plants, through boiling.

*diachylon.* An unguent made from plant juices.

*diapalma.* A plaster or bandage named for the spatula made from a palm branch that was used to stir the mixture.

*dilation.* The opening of external or internal bodily pores through heat, exercise, baths, diet, or medications.

*dispositions of the body.* The composition of the body, including temperament or the presence of occult properties, that determines susceptibility to disease.

*dropsy.* The pathological retention of water in the body that results in swelling.

*dyscrasia.* An imbalanced mixture or temperament.

*Egyptian unguent.* A compound medicine typically made from verdigris, honey, and red alum.

*electuary.* A medication in a powder form mixed with syrup or in the form of a sweet paste that is licked or taken orally.

*external causes of disease.* Environmental, behavioral, or emotional influences on the body. In Galenic medicine these are called the six non-naturals because they were considered to be distinct from the body's nature. The six non-naturals are: air, food and drink, sleep and wakefulness, exercise, evacuation and retention of fluids, and the emotions.

*faculty.* A natural power. In the body, the faculties include the actions of appetite, attraction, assimilation, digestion, retention, excretion, expulsion, and growth, which are linked to bodily functions. In medications, the faculties derive from the activities of the manifest and occult qualities of the substance.

*fomite.* Material, such as clothing, bedding, or furniture, that preserves the seeds of contagion and acts as an intermediary for transmitting disease. Mercuriale used the same word for the matter inside the body that fuels or sparks putrefaction and pestilential fevers.

*French Disease (or French Pox or French Plague).* A name for syphilis. It was called "French" because of early reports that French soldiers transmitted the disease during Charles VIII's invasion of Italy in 1494 and 1495.

*holy unguent.* A preparation or ointment believed to be especially effective, thus given the name "holy," perhaps originating in Egypt.

*humors.* Four fluids (blood, black bile, red or yellow bile, and phlegm) contained in the body. Each humor is characterized by two of the four manifest qualities (hot, cold, wet, dry). Excesses and putrefaction of humors was considered to be a common cause of disease.

*innate heat.* The heat of a living body that allows it to function, also called natural or vital heat.

*intemperance.* A qualitative disbalance of a body's natural temperament. The term can also be used for a constitution of air that is disbalanced or does not reflect the normal temperament of the season.

*internal causes of disease.* Bodily dispositions and states that lead to illness, such as temperamental imbalances and putrefactions, obstruction of passages and vessels, and discontinuity between body parts.

*lazaretto* (lazzaretto *in modern Italian*). A plague hospital or quarantine station. The word derives from a corruption of the word *Nazareth* (taken from Santa Maria di Nazareth), which is the name of an island and its church in the Venetian lagoon. The island was used to isolate the sick. In the fifteenth century, the Republic of Venice built a station on a separate island (Lazzaretto Nuovo) to quarantine incoming goods and healthy people who might have been exposed to plague.

*liniment*. A liquid medication rubbed into the skin.

*manna*. A sweet gum or resin scraped off plants. It was also referred to as aerial sugar because it was believed to be condensation from dew.

*manifest qualities*. Sensible properties, namely, hot, cold, wet, and dry. Cold and especially hot were considered to be active qualities.

*miasma*. Putrefied or rotting vapor that alters the air when mixed with it, like those arising from swamps, cemeteries, filth, and cadavers.

*Mithridates' preparation*. A complex compound medicine that, according to legend, was a universal antidote. Its invention was credited to Mithridates VI Eupator of Pontus (c. 135–63 BCE), the king of Pontus.

*mixed bodies*. Bodies composed out of mixtures of the elements as opposed to pure elements.

*noble parts*. The body's vital organs of the body, such as the brain, heart, and liver. Non-noble parts include those located in the body's extremities.

*occult quality or property*. A quality that cannot be directly sensed but can be known through experiences of its effect. A classic example is the attractive power of magnets. In Renaissance medicine, poisons, stars, and some medications were believed to possess occult qualities that accounted for their powers. Mercuriale also called these qualities and properties "arcane," "hidden," or "secret."

*orpiment*. A gold-colored mineral formed from arsenic sulfide.

*pestilential fever*. Galen, Avicenna, and others understood pestilence to be a kind of deathly fever or unnatural bodily heat. Mercuriale considered pestilential fever to be a symptom of plague but held that it also occurred distinct from plague.

*phlebotomy*. Cutting open a vein to evacuate or purge blood, synonymous with venesection.

*phlegm*. One of the four humors. Characterized by coldness and wetness and associated with the brain.

*pleurisy*. A condition consisting of pain in the chest or on the side of the torso. It is not identical to but might overlap with modern pleuritis, which is inflammation of membranes around the lungs.

*popliteal vein*. A large vein that runs down the back of the leg.

*posca*. A drink made of watered-down vinegar, sometimes with herbs infused or mixed in.

*preternatural*. Not following the ordinary course of nature. Examples of the preternatural include diseases and rare, portentous events. The word was often used to describe extreme, marvelous, or stupefying phenomena as well as abnormal bodily conditions, such as tumors or extreme fevers.

*pustules*. Open sores smaller than carbuncles or buboes that sometimes develop on the body of those afflicted by bubonic plague.

*putrefaction*. The decay or rotting of a substance caused by its internal heat being overtaken by external heat or cold, poison, or an occult quality.

*quartan fever*. A fever characterized by intervals of three days in between peaks. Thus, the fever periodically breaks on the fourth day.

*regimen*. A primary mode of preserving or restoring health by regulating behavior related to the six non-naturals.

*resolvent.* See *solutive.*

*repletion.* A bodily condition marked by a fullness or excess of blood.

*sarcocolla.* A gum resin made from *Astragalus sarcocolla*, a shrub native to Persia, used to heal wounds.

*sarcotic.* Regenerating flesh and skin.

*scabies.* A contagious skin condition that produces rashes and itching.

*scarification.* Cutting the surface of the skin or applying hot instruments to provoke blisters in order to purge the body of poisons or humors.

*simples.* Medicines made out of one substance, or the single substances used as ingredients in compound medicines. Most simples are botanic or mineral.

*solutive.* A medication that purges and eliminates humors or diseased bodily matter. The term is synonymous with resolvent.

*spirits.* Subtle material substances in the body that are responsible for its functioning. There are three bodily spirits: the animal spirit associated with the brain and sensation; the heart's vital spirit, which organizes respiration and the innate heat; and the natural spirit of the liver, which controls reproduction, nutrition, and growth.

*surgery.* Along with pharmacy and regimen, one of the three ways physicians addressed disease. Surgery for plague consisted primarily of bloodletting and excising buboes, carbuncles, and pustules.

*temperament.* A fundamental concept of Galenic medicine that refers to the mixture of the four primary qualities (hot, cold, wet, dry) of the elements (earth, water, air, fire). All humans have temperaments that reflect their physical constitution or disposition. Similarly, medications, the air, and seasons have temperaments. The ideal temperament is balanced. Disbalanced temperaments or intemperances are causes of disease, while opposites and contraries can be used to restore balances.

*tertian fever.* A fever characterized by intervals of two days in between peaks. Thus, the fever periodically breaks on the third day.

*theriac.* A complex compound medicine that originated in the ancient world and was used as an antidote and cure-all. Its ingredients included opium, cinnamon, and viper's flesh.

*venesection.* Cutting open a vein to evacuate or purge blood, synonymous with phlebotomy.

*vesicatory.* A substance, usually in the form of a paste, that provokes blisters on the skin, used to purge and evacuate harmful humors or putrefaction.

# NOTES

## INTRODUCTION

1. Paolo Preto, *Peste e società a Venezia nel 1576* (Vicenza: Neri Pozza, 1978).

2. Iain Alexander Fenlon, *The Ceremonial City: History, Memory and Myth in Renaissance Venice* (New Haven, CT: Yale University Press, 2008).

3. Samuel K. Cohn Jr., *Cultures of Plague: Medical Thinking at the End of the Renaissance* (Oxford: Oxford University Press, 2010), 95–139. Cohn provides an exhaustive account of this plague's effects and reactions to it throughout Italy.

4. Richard Palmer, "Girolamo Mercuriale and the Plague of Venice," in *Girolamo Mercuriale, medicina e cultura nell'Europa del Cinquecento*, ed. Alessandro Arcangeli and Vivian Nutton (Florence: Olschki, 2008), 51–65; Vivian Nutton, "With Benefit of Hindsight: Girolamo Mercuriale and Simone Simoni on Plague," *Medicina e storia* 11 (2006): 5–19; Cohn, *Cultures of Plague*, 177–78.

5. For Mercuriale's biography, see Giuseppe Ongaro, "Girolamo Mercuriale," in *Dizionario biografico degli Italiani* (Rome: Istituto della Enciclopedia Italiana, 2009), 73:620–25.

6. Girolamo Mercuriale, *De morbis cutaneis et omnibus corporis humani excrementis* (Venice: Meietti, 1572). The work was reprinted in various formats in 1577, 1585, 1589, 1601, 1618, and 1623.

7. Cohn, *Cultures of Plague*, 180.

8. For the publishing history of his works on practical medicine, see Nancy G. Siraisi, "*Medicina Practica*: Girolamo Mercuriale as Teacher and Textbook Author," in *Scholarly Knowledge: Textbooks in Early Modern Europe*, ed. Emidio Campi et al. (Geneva: Droz, 2008), 287–305.

9. Cohn describes him as "perhaps the most famous doctor of the last quarter of the sixteenth century," at *Cultures of Plague*, 51. Vivian Nutton calls him the "most eminent Italian professor of medicine in the last quarter of the sixteenth century," at "Greek Science in the Sixteenth-century Renaissance," in *Renaissance and Revolution: Humanists, Scholars, Craftsmen, and Natural Philosophers in Early Modern Europe*, ed. J. V. Field and Frank A. J. L. James (Cambridge: Cambridge University Press, 1993), 18.

10. Girolamo Manfredi, *Tractato de la pestilentia/Tractatus de peste*, ed. Tommaso Duranti (Bologna: CLUEB, 2008), 89–93.

11. George R. Keiser, "Two Medieval Plague Treatises and Their Afterlife in Early Modern England," *Journal of the History of Medicine and Allied Sciences* 58, no. 3 (2003): 292–324.

12. Tommaso Del Garbo, *Consiglio contr'alla peste* (Venice: Giunta, 1556); Marsilio Ficino, *Il consiglio contra la pestilentia* (Venice: Giunta, 1556). For a summary of the content of plague treatises written around the time of the Black Death, see Anna Montgomery Campbell, *The Black Death and*

*Men of Learning* (New York: Columbia University Press, 1931), 34–92. For plague treatises in the Italian tradition from the fourteenth to the sixteenth century, see Richard Palmer, "The Control of Plague in Venice and Northern Italy" (PhD diss., University of Kent at Canterbury, 1978), 87–122.

13. Raymond Chalin de Vinario, *De peste libri tres*, ed. Jacques Dalechamps (Lyon: Rouillé, 1552), 13–15.

14. Colin Jones, "Plague and Its Metaphors in Early Modern France," *Representations* 53 (Winter 1996): 97–127.

15. Marianne Pade, "Thucydides," in *Catalogus translationum et commentariorum*, ed. Virginia Brown (Washington, DC: Catholic University of America Press, 2003), 8:103–81.

16. Brian Croke, "Procopius, from Manuscripts to Books: 1400–1850," *Histos* supplement 9 (2019): 1.32.

17. *Ecclesiasticae historiae* (Paris: Estienne, 1544).

18. Ada Palmer, *Reading Lucretius in the Renaissance* (Cambridge, MA: Harvard University Press, 2014), 59–60.

19. Georg Agricola, *De peste libri tres* (Basel: Froben, 1554), 58.

20. Anthony Grafton, *What Was History? The Art of History in Early Modern Europe* (Cambridge: Cambridge, University Press, 2007), 26.

21. Lester K. Little, "Plague Historians in Lab Coats," *Past & Present* 213, no. 1 (2011): 267–90.

22. Dionysios Stathakopoulos, "Crime and Punishment: The Plague in the Byzantine Empire, 541–749," in *Plague and the End of Antiquity: The Pandemic of 541–749*, ed. Lester K. Little (Cambridge: Cambridge University Press, 2007), 105.

23. For the historiography of the three pandemics and its problems, see Merle Eisenberg and Lee Mordechai, "The Justinianic Plague and Global Pandemics: The Making of the Plague Concept," *American Historical Review* 125, no. 5 (2020): 1632–67.

24. Michelle Ziegler, "The Black Death and the Future of the Plague," *Medieval Globe* 1 (2014): 266.

25. Ziegler, "The Black Death and the Future of the Plague," 268–69.

26. For the kinds of plague, its vectors, and the frequency of pneumonic plague, see Ziegler, "The Black Death and the Future of the Plague," 259–83. For continuing questions surrounding the vectors of medieval and ancient plagues, see Eisenberg and Mordechai, "The Justinianic Plague," 1651–54. For the vectors of medieval plague in a global context, see Monica H. Green, "Taking 'Pandemic' Seriously: Making the Black Death Global," *Medieval Globe* 1 (2014): 27–61.

27. Cohn, *Cultures of Plague*, 65–73.

28. For mortality rates of the Black Death, see Ole J. Benedictow, *The Black Death 1346–1353: The Complete History* (Woodbridge: Boydell, 2004), 245–305.

29. Samuel K. Cohn Jr., "The Black Death: End of a Paradigm," *American Historical Review* 107, no. 3 (2002): 727–35.

30. The statistics are based on the Health Office's secretary Cornelio Morello. See Jane L. Stevens Crawshaw, *Plague Hospitals: Public Health for the City in Early Modern Venice* (Burlington, VT: Ashgate, 2012), 187. For a list of epidemics with death tolls in Venice from 1348 to 1631, see Palmer, "Control of Plague," 329–37. For the estimate of Venice's population in 1575, see Gordon M. Weiner, "The Demographic Effects of the Venetian Plagues of 1575–77 and 1630–31," *Genus* 26, no. 1/2 (1970): 41–57; Frederic C. Lane, *Venice: A Maritime Republic* (Baltimore: Johns Hopkins University Press, 1975), 19, 462; John Jeffries Martin, *Venice's Hidden Enemies: Italian Heretics in a Renaissance City* (Berkeley: University of California Press, 1993), 25, n. 1.

31. Alessandro Canobbio, a notary who wrote a narrative of the plague, counted 7,312 deaths in Padua; 2,977 in the lazaretto; and 2,099 in country estates. See Alessandro Canobbio, *Il successo della peste occorsa in Padova l'anno MDLXXVI* (Venice: Perchacino, 1577), fol. 34r. Around 35,000 people lived in Padua in 1575. For the estimated population in 1548 and 1604, see Karl Julius Beloch, *Storia della popolazione d'Italia*, tr. Marco Nardi (Florence: Le Lettere, 1994), 633.

32. For the historical narrative of the plague at Venice, I am greatly indebted to the archival research in Palmer, "Girolamo Mercuriale," and to the account in Cohn, *Cultures of Plague*, 124–31, 162–86. For citations to earlier accounts of Mercuriale and the debate over "true plague," see Cohn, *Cultures of Plague*, 162, n. 9.

33. For detailed descriptions of the quarantines at Venice from 1575 to 1577 and the mortality rate at the lazarettos, see Crawshaw, *Plague Hospitals*, 79–107, 189–91. For Venice's general strategy for controlling the plague in the sixteenth century as well as specifics for 1576, see Palmer, "Control of Plague," 123–49.

34. For the Venetians' hate of the quarantine, see Rocco Benedetti, *Novi avisi di Venetia ne' quali si contengono tutti i casi miserabili, che in quella al tempo della peste sono occorsi* (Urbino: Benacci, 1577), sig. A2r. For the government's economic and political concerns, see Fenlon, *The Ceremonial City*, 220; Cohn, *Cultures of Plague*, 125–26; Andrea Morosini, *Degl'istorici delle cose veneziane quali hanno scritto per pubblico decreto* (Venice: Lovisa, 1719), 6:628.

35. Cohn, *Cultures of Plague*, 82–89, 134–38, 162–86. On the development of the term *vera pestis* during the plague of 1555–1556, see Palmer, "Control of Plague," 122.

36. Palmer, "Girolamo Mercuriale," 56.

37. Benedetti, *Novi avisi*, sig. A2v.

38. Morosini, *Degl'istorici*, 6:628.

39. Morosini, *Degl'istorici*, 6:628.

40. Palmer, "Girolamo Mercuriale," 61.

41. Palmer, "Girolamo Mercuriale," 62–63.

42. Crawshaw, *Plague Hospitals*, 84–85.

43. A record of his disputations at Padua were printed; see Girolamo Zacco, *Theoremata ex variis naturalis philosophiae, ac medicinae locis deprompta per Hieronymum Zaccum patavinum disputanda* (Padua: Pasquato, 1573). He also took notes on Giacomo Zabarella's lectures on Aristotle's *Meteorology* in 1573. See Charles H. Lohr, *Latin Aristotle Commentaries. Volume II: Renaissance Authors* (Florence: Olschki, 1988), 501.

44. Crawshaw, *Plague Hospitals*, 187.

45. Jerome L. Bylebyl, "The School of Padua: Humanistic Medicine in the Sixteenth Century," in *Health, Medicine and Mortality in the Sixteenth Century*, ed. Charles Webster (Cambridge: Cambridge University Press, 1979), 335–70; Luce Giard, "Histoire de l'université et histoire du savoir: Padoue (XIVe-XVIe siècle)," *Revue de synthèse* 104 (1983): 139–69.

46. Vivian Nutton, "The Rise of Medical Humanism: Ferrara, 1464–1555," *Renaissance Studies* 11, no. 1 (1997): 2–19; John Monfasani, "The Pseudo-Aristotelian *Problemata* and Aristotle's *De animalibus* in the Renaissance," in *Natural Particulars: Nature and the Disciplines in Renaissance Europe*, ed. Anthony Grafton and Nancy Siraisi (Cambridge, MA: MIT Press 1999), 205–47.

47. Richard J. Durling, "A Chronological Census of Renaissance Editions and Translations of Galen," *Journal of the Warburg and Courtauld Institutes* 24, no. 3–4 (1961): 230–305; Gilles Maloney and Raymond Savoie, *Cinq cent ans de bibliographie hippocratique, 1473–1982* (Saint-Jean Chrysostome, Quebec: Editions du Sphinx, 1982).

48. For the growth of interest in the *Epidemics*, see Gianna Pomata, "*Praxis Historialis:* The Uses of *Historia* in Early Modern Medicine," in *Historia: Empiricism and Erudition in Early Modern Europe*, ed. Gianna Pomata and Nancy G. Siraisi (Cambridge, MA: MIT Press, 2005), 127–35; Iain M. Lonie, "The 'Paris Hippocratics': Teaching and Research in Paris in the Second Half of the Sixteenth Century," in *The Medical Renaissance of the Sixteenth Century*, ed. Roger K. French et al. (Cambridge: Cambridge University Press, 1985), 155–74; Nancy G. Siraisi, *History, Medicine, and the Traditions of Renaissance Learning* (Ann Arbor: University of Michigan Press, 2007), 72–79. For Mercuriale's editorial work, see Stefania Fortuna, "Girolamo Mercuriale editore di Galeno," in *Girolamo Mercuriale, medicina e cultura nell'Europa del Cinquecento*, ed. Alessandro Arcangeli and Vivian Nutton (Florence: Olschki, 2008), 217–31; Jacques Jouanna, "Mercuriale, commentateur et éditeur d'Hippocrate," in *Girolamo Mercuriale, medicina e cultura nell'Europa del Cinquecento*, ed. Alessandro Arcangeli and Vivian Nutton (Florence: Olschki, 2008), 269–300.

49. Girolamo Mercuriale, *Praelectiones pisanae in epidemicas Hippocratis historias* (Venice: Giunta, 1597).

50. Dag Nikolaus Hasse, *Success and Suppression: Arabic Sciences and Philosophy in the Renaissance* (Cambridge, MA: Harvard University Press, 2016). For Mercuriale's reading recommendations for ancient, medieval, and Renaissance authors, who wrote in Greek, Latin, and Arabic, see Richard J. Durling, "Girolamo Mercuriale's *De modo studendi*," *Osiris* 2nd ser. 6 (1990): 181–95.

51. Nancy G. Siraisi, "History, Antiquarianism, and Medicine: The Case of Girolamo Mercuriale," *Journal of the History of Ideas* 64, no. 2 (2003): 231–51; Ginette Vagenheim, "Una collaborazione tra antiquario ed erudito: I disegni e le epigrafi di Pirro Ligorio nel *De arte gymnastica* di Girolamo Mercuriale," in *Girolamo Mercuriale, medicina e cultura nell'Europa del Cinquecento*, ed. Alessandro Arcangeli and Vivian Nutton (Florence: Olschki, 2008), 127–57.

52. Girolamo Mercuriale, *Variarum lectionum libri quatuor* (Venice: Meietti, 1570), fol. 79r.

53. Mercuriale, *Variarum*, fols. 115r–16r.

54. Nancy G. Siraisi, *Avicenna in Renaissance Italy: The Canon and Medical Teaching in Italian Universities after 1500* (Princeton, NJ: Princeton University Press, 1987).

55. Linda Deer Richardson, "The Generation of Disease: Occult Causes and Diseases of the Total Substance," in *The Medical Renaissance of the Sixteenth Century*, ed. Andrew Wear et al. (Cambridge: Cambridge University Press, 1985), 175–94. For Fernel's theory of plague and occult causes, see Jean Fernel, *On the Hidden Causes of Things*, ed. and tr. John M. Forrester (Leiden: Brill, 2005), (2.12) 562–94.

56. Hiro Hirai, *Le concept de semence dans les théories de la matière à la Renaissance* (Turnhout: Brepols, 2005), 73–80; Vivian Nutton, "The Reception of Fracastoro's Theory of Contagion," *Osiris* 2nd ser. 6 (1990): 196–234; Concetta Pennuto, *Simpatia, fantasia e contagio: Il pensiero medico e il pensiero filosofico di Girolamo Fracastoro* (Rome: Edizioni di Storia e Letteratura, 2008).

57. Cohn, *Cultures of Plague*, 195–200.

58. Cohn, *Cultures of Plague*, 166–67.

59. Annibale Raimondo, *Discorso nel quale chiaramente si conosce la viva et vera cagione, che ha generato le fiere infermità* (Padua: s.n., 1576).

60. Giovanni Filippo Ingrassia, *Informatione del pestifero, et contagioso morbo* (Palermo: Mayda, 1576).

61. For Ingrassia's biography see Cesare Preti, "Giovanni Filippo Ingrassia," in *Dizionario biografico degli Italiani* (Rome: Istituto della Enciclopedia Italiana, 2004), 62:396–99.

62. See for example, Niccolò Massa, *Ragionamento sopra le infermità, che vengono dall'aere pestilentiale del presente anno* (Venice: Ziletti, 1556), fol. 13r–13v; Leonardo Fioravanti, *Del regimento della*

*peste* (Venice: Ravenoldo, 1565), fol. 36r–36v; Vittorio Bonagente, *Decem problemata de peste* (Venice: Valgrisi, 1556); Gabriele Falloppio, *De bubone pestilentiali* in *Opuscula* (Padua: Bertelli, 1566).

63. Giancarlo Cerasoli and Brunella Garavini, "Il codice di Girolamo Mercuriale con le anno-tazioni sulle condizioni climatiche di Padova nel 1577–1578 durante la peste (BCR, Cod. 467)," *Ravenna studi e ricerche* 11, no. 2 (2004): 131–51.

64. In his later commentary on the *Epidemics*, Mercuriale for the most part eschewed the word *constitutio*, instead using *historia* for each of the case histories. See Mercuriale, *In epidemicas Hippocratis historias*.

65. For estimated suspected plague deaths by month in Venice for 1576, see Crawshaw, *Plague Hospitals*, plate 26. Deaths continued to be counted through December, with significant numbers in July, August, September, and October.

66. Arist. *Meteor.* 4.1, 379a17–19.

67. On miasma in the Hippocratic corpus and afterward, see Jacques Jouanna, "Air, Miasma, and Contagion in the Time of Hippocrates and the Survival of Miasmas in Post-Hippocratic Medi-cine (Rufus of Ephesus, Galen and Palladius)," in *Greek Medicine from Hippocrates to Galen: Selected Papers* (Leiden: Brill, 2012), 121–36.

68. Concetta Pennuto, "Girolamo Mercuriale e la dottrina dei giorni critici," in *Girolamo Mercuriale, medicina e cultura nell'Europa del Cinquecento*, ed. Alessandro Arcangeli and Vivian Nutton (Florence: Olschki, 2008), 301–17.

69. For example, see Raymond Chalin de Vinario, *De peste libri tres*, ed. Jacques Dalechamps (Lyon: Rouillé, 1552), 13–21. Mercuriale cited Raymond's treatise.

70. Jon Arrizabalaga, "Facing the Black Death: Perceptions and Reactions of University Med-ical Practitioners," in *Practical Medicine: Salerno to the Black Death*, ed. Luis García Ballester et al. (Cambridge: Cambridge University Press, 1994), 252–54.

71. R. P. Duncan-Jones, "The Antonine Plague Revisited," *Arctos* 52 (2018): 41–72; Kyle Harper, "Pandemics and Passages to Late Antiquity: Rethinking the Plague of c. 249–270 Described by Cyprian," *Journal of Roman Archaeology* 28 (2015): 223; Michael McCormick, "Rats, Communications, and Plague: Toward an Ecological History," *Journal of Interdisciplinary History* 34, no. 1 (2003): 1–25.

72. On the plague that struck Constantinople in 746–747 CE, see David Turner, "The Pol-itics of Despair: The Plague of 746–747 and Iconoclasm in the Byzantine Empire," *Annual of the British School at Athens* 85 (1990): 419–34.

73. For Mercuriale's historical analysis of plague, see Nancy G. Siraisi, *History, Medicine, and the Traditions of Renaissance Learning* (Ann Arbor: University of Michigan Press, 2007), 102–5.

74. For Fracastoro's influence, including on Mercuriale, see Nutton, "Reception of Fracas-toro's Theory."

75. These theories are outlined in a letter Girolamo Fracastoro wrote to Giovanni Battista Della Torre found at Girolamo Fracastoro, *La dottrina fracastoriana del contagium vivum*, ed. Fran-cesco Pellegrini (Verona: Valdonega, 1950), 35–54.

76. On the six non-naturals, see Sandra Cavallo and Tessa Storey, *Healthy Living in Renais-sance Italy* (Oxford: Oxford University Press, 2013).

77. Marion Maria Ruisinger, "Die Pestarztmaske im Deutschen Medizinhistorischen Museum Ingolstadt," *NTM Zeitschrift für Geschichte der Wissenschaft, Technik und Medizin* 28 (June 2020): 235–52.

78. Pier Andrea Mattioli, *Commentarii, in libros sex Pedacii Dioscoridis Anazarbei, De medica materia* (Venice: Valgrisi, 1554).

79. Christiane Nockels Fabbri, "Treating Medieval Plague: The Wonderful Virtues of Theriac," *Early Science and Medicine* 12, no. 3 (2007): 247–83. Nockels Fabbri suggests that the opium contained in theriac might have relieved some of the plague victims' symptoms.

80. For the methods and practices of Venetian pharmacists, see Richard Palmer, "Pharmacy in the Republic of Venice in the Sixteenth Century," in *The Medical Renaissance of the Sixteenth Century*, ed. Andrew Wear et al. (Cambridge: Cambridge University Press, 1985), 100–117; Valentina Pugliano, "Pharmacy, Testing, and the Language of Truth in Renaissance Italy," *Bulletin of the History of Medicine* 91, no. 2 (2017): 233–73.

81. Filippo De Vivo, "Pharmacies as Centres of Communication in Early Modern Venice," *Renaissance Studies* 21, no. 4 (2007): 505–21.

82. Brian W. Ogilvie, *The Science of Describing: Natural History in Renaissance Europe* (Chicago: University of Chicago Press, 2006), 70–72.

83. Girolamo Mercuriale, *De compositione medicamentorum* (Venice: Giunta, 1590).

84. Erik Heinrichs, "The Live Chicken Treatment for Buboes," *Bulletin of the History of Medicine* 91, no. 2 (2017): 210–32.

85. Cohn, *Cultures of Plague*, 15–18.

86. Martin, *Venice's Hidden Enemies*, 211–14.

87. Cohn, *Cultures of Plague*, 192–93.

88. Andrea Gratiolo, *Discorso di peste* (Venice: Polo, 1576), 3.

89. Craig Martin, *Subverting Aristotle: Religion, History, and Philosophy in Early Modern Science* (Baltimore: Johns Hopkins University Press, 2014), 51–85.

90. Bassiano Lando, *De origine et causa pestis patavinae, anni 1555* (Venice: Griffio, 1555), sigs. C2r–C2v; Palmer, "Control of Plague," 311.

91. Jonathan Seitz, *Witchcraft and Inquisition in Early Modern Venice* (Cambridge: Cambridge University Press, 2011), 187–94.

92. Giuseppe Ongaro and Elda Martellozzo Forin, "Girolamo Mercuriale e lo Studio di Padova," in *Girolamo Mercuriale, medicina e cultura nell'Europa del Cinquecento*, ed. Alessandro Arcangeli and Vivian Nutton (Florence: Olschki, 2008), 29–50.

93. Hannah Marcus, "What the Plague Can Teach Us about the Coronavirus," *New York Times,* March 1, 2020, https://www.nytimes.com/2020/03/01/opinion/coronavirus-italy.html (accessed October 1, 2020).

94. John M. Barry, "The Single Most Important Lesson from the 1918 Influenza," *New York Times,* March 17, 2020, https://www.nytimes.com/2020/03/17/opinion/coronavirus-1918-spanish-flu.html (accessed October 1, 2020).

95. Edward Watts, "What Rome Learned from the Deadly Antonine Plague of 165 A.D.," *Smithsonian Magazine*, April 28, 2020, https://www.smithsonianmag.com/history/what-rome-learned-deadly-antonine-plague-165-d-180974758/ (accessed October 1, 2020).

96. Mark Honigsbaum, "Revisiting the 1957 and 1968 Influenza Pandemics," *Lancet* 395, no. 10240 (2020): 1824–26.

97. David S. Jones, "COVID-19, History, and Humility," *Centaurus* 62, no. 2 (2020): 370–80.

98. Palmer, "Control of Plague," 143.

99. For the possible effectiveness of Venetian sanitary cordons in the seventeenth and eighteenth centuries, see Katerina Konstantinidou et al. "Venetian Rule and Control of Plague Epidemics on the Ionian Islands During the 17th and 18th Centuries," *Emerging Infectious Diseases* 15, no. 1 (2009): 39–43. For the potential mitigation of plague through quarantines and sanitary cordons in early modern Italy in general, see John Henderson, "The Invisible Enemy: Fighting the Plague in Early Modern Italy," *Centaurus* 62, no. 2 (2020): 263–74.

100. Palmer, "Control of Plague," 145–48.

101. Crawshaw, *Plague Hospitals*, 79–80.

102. For the publishing history of Mercuriale's works, see Siraisi, *"Medicina Practica."*

## ON PESTILENCE

1. Girolamo Zacco was a physician at Padua, where he had studied. He became part of the Paduan College of Physicians around 1574. See Palmer, "Girolamo Mercuriale," 63, n. 60. Zacco's disputations given at Padua were printed shortly before; see Zacco, *Theoremata*.

2. Gonfalonier of the Holy Roman Church was a military and political position of the Papal States. Boncompagni held this position under the papacy of Gregory XIII. Boncompagni was Gregory's illegitimate son.

3. Sperone Speroni (1500–1588) was a literary and philosophical figure from Padua.

4. That is, March 1, 1577.

5. The reference seems to be to Simplicius, *In Aristotelis physicorum libros quattuor priores commentaria*, 1. prooem. in *Commentaria in Aristotelem graeca*, vol. 9, ed. Hermann Diels (Berlin: Reimer, 1882), 5. Simplicius' proemium was found in many of the manuscripts of Themistius and translated under his name in the Renaissance edition made by Ermolao Barbaro; see: Themistius, *Paraphrasis*, tr. Ermolao Barbaro (Venice: Scoto, 1559), 33.

6. Mercuriale took the term "constitution" from the Hippocratic *Epidemics*. The term refers to the general circumstances of a given place, with particular emphasis on meteorological conditions and the "constitution of the air." As such, the term also refers to a particular case history of an epidemic that includes a description of its underlying causes and development.

7. This list of chapters follows the actual chapters, not the printed list (sigs. *3v–*4r) that skips chapter 7 and erroneously counts only twenty-nine chapters.

8. Carbuncles, which are discussed in detail in chapters 29 and 30, are boils that are characteristic of bubonic plague.

9. Gal. *Diff. Resp.* 2.7, 7.850–51K; Gal. *Febr. Diff.* 1.6, 7.289–91K; Thuc. 2.49; Lucr. 6.1196–98. Thucydides and Lucretius wrote about the plague of Athens that took place from 430 to 426 BCE.

10. Hom. *Il.* 1.50–53; Hp. *De flat.* 6, 6.98L; Arist. *HA* 8.19, 602b11–15.

11. For the vulnerability of women and children in this plague, see Crawshaw, *Plague Hospitals*, 100–103.

12. Plin. *NH* 7.50.170.

13. For the plague's effects on the poor see Cohn, *Cultures of Plague*, 208–37.

14. For a discussion of the identity of the man and how he entered Venice, see Palmer, "Control of Plague," 211–13.

15. Richard Palmer pointed out that this chronology is self-serving since it suggests that the plague only took hold after Mercuriale had left Venice around the start of July, when in fact the disease grew significantly in June when he was still there. See Palmer, "Girolamo Mercuriale," 60–63.

16. Gal. *Hipp. 1 Epid.* praef. 17a.2K; Hp. *Acut.* 5, (2) 2.232–34L; Hp. *De flat.* 6, 6.96–98L.

17. Hp. *Epid.* 1.5–10, (4) 2.616–32L.

18. Lucr. 6.1114–17.

19. Gal. *Hipp. 3 Epid.* 3.20–21, 17a.667–68K.

20. Basil, *Homilia in Psalmum primum*, 6 in *Patrologiae cursus completus: Series graeca*, ed. J.-P. Migne (Paris: Migne, 1857), vol. 29, col. 225.

21. Thuc. 2.47, 2.51.

22. Avicenna, *Canon* 4.1.4.1–5. Avicenna (d. 1037), or Abū ʿAlī al-Ḥusayn ibn ʿAbdallāh ibn Sīnā, was a philosopher and physician from Bukhara, which is in present-day Uzbekistan. It was capital of the Samanid Empire. His *Canon* was a fundamental textbook for teaching medicine in medieval and Renaissance universities.

23. Arist. *Prob.* 1.7, 859b15–20. The authorship of the *Problemata* is not entirely resolved, although at least portions of it are no longer held to be by Aristotle but by his followers at the Lyceum. In the sixteenth century, some scholars doubted its authenticity, although Mercuriale, like many others, seems to have accepted it as genuine.

24. Arist. *Prob.* 7.4, 886b4–8; Arist. *Prob.* 1.7, 859b16–17.

25. Gal. *Febr. Diff.* 1.3, 7.279K.

26. Procop. *Pers.* 2.22.23. In this passage, Procopius was writing about the bubonic plague that struck Constantinople beginning in 541–542 CE.

27. Gregory of Nyssa, *De pauperis amandis oratio II* in *Patrologiae cursus completus: Series graeca*, ed. J.-P. Migne (Paris: Migne, 1863), vol. 46, cols. 481–84; Matthew 25.40. Gregory of Nyssa (c. 335–395 CE) was one of the Cappadocian fathers and wrote numerous works on theology.

28. Hp. *Acut.* 5, (2) 2.232–34L.

29. Gal. *Hipp. 1 Epid.* praef., 17a.11–12K.

30. Arist. *Prob.* 1.7, 859b18–20.

31. Gal. *Febr. Diff.* 1.3, 7.279K.

32. Gregory of Nyssa, *De pauperis amandis oratio II*, vol. 46, cols. 481–84.

33. Arist. *Prob.* 7.4, 886b4–8.

34. Hp. *Acut.* 5, (2) 2.232–34L.

35. Gal. *Hipp. 3 Epid.* 3.20–21, 17a.667–68K.

36. Arist. *Prob.* 1.7, 859b15–20. Theodore Gaza translated μάλιστα as *praecipue*. The Greek word "μάλιστα" means "most of all," the Latin word "praecipue" means "chiefly" or "principally." For Gaza's translation, see Aristotle, *Problematum Aristotelis sectiones duaedequadraginta*, tr. Theodore Gaza (Lyon: Mirallietum, 1550), 3.

37. Gal. *Hipp. 3 Epid.* 3.57, 17a.709K; Gal. *Praes. Puls.* 3.4 9.359K.

38. Here, Mercuriale seems to have been referring to the use of the word σηπεδών (decay) instead of the more technical σῆψις (putrefaction) in Hippocrates' description of a deathly epidemic at Hp. *Epid.* 3.4, 3.64L. Galen used σηπεδών at Gal. *Temp.* 1.4, 1.532K to describe an extreme putrefaction or decay while citing Hippocrates' *Epidemics* 3.

39. Jean Fernel, *On the Hidden Causes of Things*, ed. and tr. John M. Forrester (Leiden: Brill, 2005), (2.12) 562–94. Jean Fernel (1497–1558) influentially devised a Platonic understanding of the causes of some diseases to be occult celestial qualities.

40. Donato Antonio Altomare, *De medendis febribus ars medica* (Venice: De Maria, 1562), 591–608. Altomare (d. c. 1566), a Neapolitan physician, published numerous works on Galenic medicine.

41. Gal. *Loc. Affect.* 6.5, 8.421–23K.

42. Avicenna, *Canon* 1.3.5.1; Gal. *Hipp. 1 Epid.* 1.1, 17a.13K.

43. Gal. *Hipp. Prog.* 1.1.4, 18b.17K; Avicenna, *Metaphysica, sive eius prima philosophia* (Venice: Scoto, 1495), 10.1, sig. I4r; Avenzoar, *Liber theisir* in *Colliget Averrois . . . Theizir Abynzoar morbos omnes* (Venice: Scoto, 1542), fol. 39r. Avenzoar is the Latinized name of Abū Marwān ibn Zuhr (d. 1162), an Andalusian physician. His *Theisir*, which was printed many times in the first half of the sixteenth century, discussed therapy and dietetics. For Avicenna, Mercuriale's text reads "XI. Metaph." but there is no book 11 of Avicenna's *Metaphysics*. I have read the text as "X.I Metaph," where a relevant passage is found.

44. Gal. *Cib.* 1, 6:750–51K; Gal. *Febr. Diff.* 1.3, 7.279K.

45. Altomare, *De medendis febribus*, 591–608.

46. Hp. *Epid.* 2.4.3, 5.126L; Hp. *Epid.* 6.4.11, 5.133L.

47. Philost. *VA* 4.4, 8.7; Philost. *Her.* 33.14. Apollonius of Tyana (first century CE) was cred-ited with performing various wonders during his life, which was largely spent traveling. Philostra-tus' biography is the primary source for his life.

48. On the Ferrarese earthquakes of the 1570s, see Craig Martin, *Renaissance Meteorology: Pomponazzi to Descartes* (Baltimore: Johns Hopkins University Press, 2011), 60–79.

49. A supernova appeared in November of 1572. Tycho Brahe discussed it in his *De nova et nullius aevi memoria prius visa stella* (Copenhagen: Laurentius Benedictus, 1573).

50. Mercuriale, like most Renaissance philosophers and physicians, accepted that some insects and invertebrates are spontaneously generated out of decaying matter.

51. Mercuriale was likely referring to conjoined twins born in Venice's Ghetto on May 26, 1575. See David B. Ruderman, "Out of the Mouths of Babes and Sucklings," in *Monsters and Monstrosity in Jewish History: From the Middle Ages to Modernity*, ed. Iris Idelson-Shein and Christian Wiese (London: Bloomsbury, 2019), 213–14.

52. Andrea Gratiolo, a physician from Salò, wrote there was an eclipse of the sun in April of 1575 but denied it could be the cause of the plague. See Gratiolo, *Discorso*, 19–20. Similarly, Giovanni Filippo Ingrassia, a physician trained in Padua who became *protomedico* of Sicily, main-tained that there was an eclipse of the sun on November 13, 1575, but dismissed any link to the plague. See Ingrassia, *Informatione*, 18–19.

53. Hp. *Epid.* 2.1.1, 5.72L; Ov. *Met.* 7.552–633; Thuc. 2.49; Lucr. 6.1138–285; Procop. *Pers.* 2.22–23; Gal. *Libr. Propr.* 1, 19.15K; Gal. *Libr. Propr.* 2, 19.18K; Gal. *Simp. Med.* 9.1.4, 12.189–92K; Evagrius, *Historia ecclesiastica*, 4.29; Nicephorus Callistus, *Historia ecclesiastica*, 17.18 in *Patrologiae cursus completus: Series graeca*, ed. J.-P. Migne (Paris: Migne, 1865), vol. 147, cols. 265–68. Evagrius Scholasticus (sixth century CE) and Nicephorus Callistus Xanthopulus (c. 1250–c. 1335) were both ecclesiastical historians who wrote in Greek. Evagrius lived during the Justinianic plague.

54. Thuc. 2.49.

55. Hp. *Epid.* 2.1.1, 5.72L.

56. Plin. *NH* 11.32.93–94.

57. Fernel, *On Hidden Causes*, (2.12) 562–94.

58. Altomare, *De medendis febribus*, 586–90.

59. Arist. *GA* 2.3, 736b33–37a7.

60. Gal. *Simp. Med.* 9.1.4, 12.191–92K; Gal. *Simp. Med.* 10.1.15, 12.285K. Armenian bole is a clay that was prominent in ancient, medieval, and early modern pharmacology. Theriac is a com-plex compound medicine that originated in the ancient world and was used as an antidote and cure-all. Galen wrote about and prepared theriac. Its ingredients included opium, cinnamon, and viper's flesh.

61. Avicenna, *Canon* 1.3.5.1; 4.1.4.1; Hp. *Morb.* 4.20–21, (51–52) 7.584–94L. Mercuriale attributed *De morbis* to Polybus, a follower of Hippocrates; see Girolamo Mercuriale, *Censura ope-rum Hippocratis* in *Hippocratis Coi opera quae extant graece et latine*, ed. G. Mercuriale (Venice: Giunta, 1588), 11.

62. Gal. *Hipp. Nat. Hom.* 2.4, 15.121–22K.

63. This story is recounted in Julius Capitolinus, *Historia Augusta*, Lucius Verus 8.2.

64. Ammianus, *Res gestae*, 23.6.23.

65. Arist. *Long.* 5, 466a24–27; Arist. *Prob.* 25.20, 939b27–32.

66. Arist. *Meteor.* 4.1, 379a14–16.

67. Hp. *De flat.* 6, 6.98L. Here, Mercuriale used the Greek word μιάσματα.

68. Arist. *Prob.* 25.20, 939b29–31.

69. Mercuriale wrote the Greek word κατάστασις.

70. Gal. *Temp.* 1.4, 1:531K.

71. Avicenna, *Canon* 4.1.4.1.

72. Hp. *Prog.* 1, 2.112L.

73. Hp. *Nat. Mul.* 1, 7:312L. Here, Mercuriale employed the Greek phrasing τὸ θεῖον and ἀπὸ τῶν θειῶν.

74. Hp. *Morb.* 4.20–21, (51–52) 7.584–94L; Stephanus of Athens, *In Hippocratis Prognosticum commentaria III*, ed. and trans. John M. Duffy, in *Corpus medicorum graecorum*, vol. 11.1.2 (Berlin: Akademie-Verlag, 1983), 1.17, 62–64. Taddeo Alderotti, *Expositiones in divinum pronosticorum Ipocratis librum* (Venice: Giunta, 1527), fol. 197v. Taddeo Alderotti (c. 1220–1295) taught theoretical medicine at Bologna.

75. Avicenna, *Canon* 1.3.5.1, Avicenna, *Canon* 4.1.4.1.

76. Hp. *Carn.* 2, 8.584L. Modern interpreters have not accepted Mercuriale's emendation of Περὶ σαρκῶν to Περὶ αρχῶν for the title of *On Fleshes*.

77. Hp. *Epid.* 2.1.4, 5.74L.

78. Plat. *Epin.* 977e4–5; Arist. *GA* 2.3, 736b33–37a7.

79. Hom. *Il.* 1.43–53.

80. Gal. *Temp.* 1.4, 1.529–32K.

81. Ammianus, *Res gestae*, 19.4.2.

82. Verg. *Aen.* 3.135–46.

83. Mercuriale possibly referred to Liv. 1.31 and the plague that killed Tullus Hostilius in 642 BCE, although there is no mention of drought. But see also Liv. 5.31. Nicephorus Callistus, *Historia ecclesiastica*, 15.10, vol. 147, cols. 33–36.

84. Avenzoar, *Liber theisir*, 39r.

85. Mercuriale perhaps was referring to a plague supposedly caused by a cold winter reported in a catalog of plagues in Gratiolo, *Discorso di peste*, 123.

86. Arist. *Prob.* 1.21, 862a4–9.

87. According to medieval and Renaissance natural philosophers and astrologers, the heavens influence the earth by their motion, light, and influence. Influence typically refers to an occult power or quality.

88. Arist. *Prob.* 1.21, 862a4–9.

89. Hp. *Aph.* 3.8, 4.488L. Auster is a southerly wind.

90. Gal. *Febr. Diff.* 1.6, 7.289K. Perhaps Mercuriale was referring to the passage found at Hp. *De flat.* 5, 6.96L.

91. Fernel, *On Hidden Causes*, (2.12) 562–94.

92. Avicenna, *Canon* 4.1.4.1.

93. Gal. *Febr. Diff.* 1.7, 7.295–96K.

94. Evagrius, *Historia ecclesiastica* 4.29.

95. Avicenna, *Canon* 4.1.4.1.

96. Jacques Despars, *Fen prima quarti Canonis Avicennae principis cum explanatione Jacobi de Partibus* (Lyon: Lascaris, 1498), comm. 4.1.4.1, fol. 117r. Jacques Despars (c. 1380–1458), or Desparts, served as physician to Charles VII.

97. Rhazes, *Liber ad Almansorem* (Venice: De Leuco, 1508), 4.25, fol. 20r; 10.28, fol. 54v.

98. Ov. *Met.* 7.552–633.

99. Thuc. 2.51–52; Lucr. 6.250–51.

100. Plut. *Cam.* 43. Marcus Furius Camillus (c. 446–c. 335 BCE) was a Roman politician and soldier who was acclaimed dictator multiple times.

101. Eusebius, *En damus chronicon divinum plane opus* (Basel: Henricpetri, 1529), fol. 74v. Eusebius wrote that there was a plague in Rome in 80 CE.

102. Procop. *Pers.* 2.23.2.

103. Leo III the Isaurian was Byzantine emperor from 717 to 741. There was a large outbreak of plague under the rule of his son Constantine V in 746 and 747. See Nicephorus, *Breviarum* 65 in *Patrologiae cursus completus: Series graeca*, ed. J.-P. Migne (Paris: Migne, 1865), vol. 100, col. 496. The twelfth-century chronicler Godfrey of Viterbo wrote that the plague occurred under Leo and that three hundred thousand died. See Godfrey of Viterbo, *Pantheon sive Universitatis libri, qui chronici appellantur, XX* (Basel: Parcus, 1559), cols. 500–501.

104. Platina, *Historia de vitis pontificum romanorum* (Venice: Tramezzino, 1562), fol. 125r. Platina was the pen name for the humanist scholar Bartolomeo Sacchi (1421–1481). Benedict VIII was pope from 1012 to 1024.

105. Despars, *Fen prima quarti Canonis*, comm. 4.1.4.1, fol. 116v. Despars, although he witnessed two plagues, was born after the plague described here.

106. Marco Antonio Sabellico, *Historiae rerum venetarum ab urbe condita libri XXXIII* (Basel: Episcopius, 1556), 373–74. Sabellico (d. 1506) a humanist scholar wrote a history of Venice as well as a universal history.

107. Liv. 4.52. The name of the first consul was Quintus Fabius Vibulanus Ambustus. They held the consulship in 412 BCE.

108. Gal. *Simp. Med.* 10.1.15, 12.285K; Gal. *Usu Part.* 3.5, 1.137–38K.

109. Leontios ruled from 695 to 698. Theophanes the Confessor (c. 760–c. 817) reported that the plague struck Constantinople at the end of his rule. Theophanes, *Chronographia* 309 in *Patrologiae cursus completus: Series graeca*, ed. J.-P. Migne (Paris: Migne, 1863), vol. 108, col. 753.

110. Perhaps this is an ironic reference to himself. His lectures on poisons were published in 1584. Girolamo Mercuriale, *De venenis et morbis venenosis tractatus* (Padua: Meietti, 1584).

111. Arist. *Prob.* 7.8, 687a33–37; [pseudo] Alexander of Aphrodisias, *Prob. phys.* 2.42, in *Physici et medici graeci minores*, ed. Julius L. Ideler (Berlin: Reimer, 1841), 1:64.

112. The word "fomite" literally refers to tinder or kindling. Mercuriale used the term, following Girolamo Fracastoro, to denote the matter, such as clothing, bedding, or furniture, that preserves and acts as an intermediary for contagion.

113. Gal. *Febr. Diff.* 1.3, 7.279K.

114. Arist. *Prob.* 7.8, 387a27–33.

115. Gal. *Simp. Med.* 3.23, 11.609–10K.

116. Plin. *NH* 7.55.189.

117. Leviticus 13.47–52.

118. Leviticus 14.39–42.

119. Girolamo Fracastoro, *De sympathia et antipathia rerum liber unus. De contagione et contagiosis morbis et curatione libri III* (Venice: Giunta, 1546), 2.8, fol. 46r. Fracastoro taught at Padua and served as papal physician to Paul III. He coined the term syphilis and developed a theory of transmission of disease based on the concept of contagion through sympathy. Mercuriale, like many of his contemporaries, adopted parts of Fracastoro's theory of contagion.

120. Hdt. 5.89.

121. Marsilio Ficino, *Il consiglio contra la pestilentia* (Venice: Giunta, 1556), 76.

122. Hp. *Int.* 19, 7.214L. The Hippocratic tradition held that a great vein ran down the length of the body's left side.

123. Thphr. *HP* 9.16.5.

124. Gal. *Loc. Affect.* 6.5, 8.423–24K; Avicenna, *Canon* 4.6.4.7.

125. Albertus Magnus, *De animalibus libri XXVI*, ed. Hermann Stadler (Münster: Aschendorff, 1916), 7.2.2, 1:543. Albertus Magnus (c. 1200–1280) was a Dominican friar and philosopher who wrote expositions on Aristotle.

126. Albucasis, *Liber theoricae nec non practicae* (Augsburg: Grimm, Sigmund & Wirsung, 1519), fol. 134v. Albucasis is the Latinized name of Abū l-Qāsim Khalaf az Zahrāwī (936–1013), or Al-Zahrawi, who was best known for his work on surgery that circulated throughout Europe during the Middle Ages.

127. Fracastoro, *De sympathia et antipathia*, 1.4, fol. 30r.

128. Evagrius, *Historia ecclesiastica* 4.29.

129. His discussion of this topic is found in the treatment of the French Disease in Girolamo Mercuriale, *Medicina practica* (Frankfurt: Schönwetter, 1602), 429. This volume was based on lectures Mercuriale gave at Padua. The French Disease, or the French Pox or French Plague, was a name used for syphilis, which emerged in Naples in 1494 and 1495, while the city was occupied by French soldiers.

130. Lucr. 6.1090–97; Fracastoro, *De sympathia et antipathia*, 2.8, fols. 45v–46r.

131. Hp. *De flat.* 6, 6.98L.

132. Here, Mercuriale used the Greek word μιάσματα.

133. Evagrius, *Historia ecclesiastica* 4.29; Nicephorus Callistus, *Historia ecclesiastica*, 17.18, vol. 147, cols. 265–68.

134. Dion. Hal. *Antiquitates romanae* 4.69.2; Gentile da Foligno, *De febribus. Expositio in prima fen quarti Canonis Avicennae* (Venice: Giunta, 1526), comm. 4.1.4.1, fol. 119v. Gentile taught medicine at Bologna, Siena, and Perugia. He died while treating the plague in 1348.

135. Fernel, *On Hidden Causes*, (2.12) 578–80.

136. Nicephorus Callistus, *Historia ecclesiastica*, 6.20, vol. 146, col. 1169; Cyprianus, *De mortalitate*, 16 in *Patrologiae cursus completus: Series latina*, ed. J.-P. Migne (Paris: Migne, 1844), col. 593. Cyprian, the bishop of Carthage, described the plague that began in 249 CE, which is sometimes referred to as the Plague of Cyprian.

137. App. *Ill.* 1.4.

138. Leviticus 15.19–33; Hes. *Op.* 753–54.

139. Tac. *Ann.* 15.43.

140. The denial of the continual bad state of air at Padua is found at Canobbio, *Il successo della peste*, fols. 18r–19r. He contended the plague stopped when Auster arrived. Similar denials of the role of universally corrupted air as the cause of the plague in Desenzano del Garda, where the air was described as pure, limpid, clear, and not cloudy is found in Gratiolo, *Discorso di peste*, 20–22. He maintained that the air at Padua was also subtle during this period.

141. Gal. *Temp.* 1.4, 1:531K.

142. Hp. *Epid.* 2.1.1, 5.72L.

143. Fernel, *On Hidden Causes*, (2.12) 564–66.

144. Gal. *Febr. Diff.* 1.6, 7.293K.

145. Hp. *Morb.* 4.3, (34) 7.544–48L; Thphr. *HP* 8.2.11; [pseudo] Mesue, *Canones universales* in *Opera* (Venice: Giunta, 1570), fol. 13r–13v. Mesue is the Latinized name of Yūḥannā ibn

Māsawayh (777–857). He was credited with having written works on simples that were greatly influential in medieval Europe.

146. Gal. *Libr. Propr.* 2, 19.18K; Gal. *Hipp. 6 Epid.* 1.29 17a.885K. Galen witnessed the Antonine plague that lasted from 165 to 180 CE. Evagrius reported Philostratus as writing this at *Historia ecclesiastica* 4.29. Philostratus lived from c. 170 to c. 250 CE.

147. Despars, *Fen prima quarti Canonis*, comm. 4.1.4.1, fol. 116v.

148. Evagrius, *Historia ecclesiastica* 4.29.

149. Thuc. 2.54–55.

150. Elia Capriolo, *Chronica de rebus Brixianorum* (Brescia: Arundi, 1505), fol. 13v. Renaissance scholars often referred to Marcus Aurelius Antoninus (121–180 CE), the emperor and philosopher, as Marcus Antoninus or Marcus Antonius.

151. Matteo Villani, *Cronica. Con la continuazione di Filippo Villani*, ed. Giuseppe Porta (Parma: Fondazione Pietro Bembo, U. Guanda, 1995), 1.2, 1:10–11. Matteo Villani (c. 1285–1363) was a Florentine historian whose *Chronicles* included a detailed account of the plague of 1348.

152. Plin. *NH* 2.98.211.

153. Gal. *Aliment. Fac.* 2.6, 6:569K.

154. Gal. *Usu Part.* 8.6, 1:448K.

155. Sen. *NQ* 6.27.4.

156. Hp. *Epid.* 6.7.1, 5.330–36L.

157. Hp. *Epid.* 6.7.1, 5.334L.

158. The separation of Venice as a quarantine measure is described at Benedetti, *Novi avisi di Venetia*, sig. B2v.

159. The Abbey of Santa Giustina is a Benedictine basilica in Padua where there was a monastery. The Basilica of Saint Anthony of Padua, known as *il Santo*, is an important Franciscan complex.

160. Raymond, *De peste*, 49. Raymond's treatise was written around 1382. He was based in Avignon.

161. Avicenna, *Canon* 4.1.4.1.

162. Fernel, *On Hidden Causes*, (2.12) 566.

163. Plut. *Per.* 34.3–4.

164. Julius Capitolinus, *Historia Augusta*, Lucius Verus 8.1. Lucius Verus was emperor, together with Marcus Aurelius from 161 to 169 CE.

165. Guglielmo Cortusi, *De novitatibus Padue et Lombardie* in *Rerum italicarum scriptores*, ed. Lodovico Antonio Muratori (Milan: Società Palatina, 1728), vol. 12, col. 926. Cortusi indicated that the person was a foreigner without identifying him as being from Venice.

166. The term Achilles' argument refers to an argument that is so strong that it cannot be refuted or overturned and is thereby considered invincible.

167. Gal. *Febr. Diff.* 1.3, 7.279K.

168. Dion. Hal. *Antiquitates romanae* 2.54.1; Plut. *Rom.* 24.1; Zonaras, *Epitome historiarum* 2.22. Joannes Zonaras (twelfth century) was a Byzantine historian.

169. Despars, *Fen prima quarti Canonis*, comm. 4.1.4.2, fol. 118r.

170. Gal. *Simp. Med.* 9.1.4, 12.191K; Avicenna, *Canon* 4.1.4.2.

171. Hp. *Morb.* 1.29, 6.198L; Gal. *Hipp. Aph.* 4.48, 17b.728–29K.

172. Avicenna, *Canon* 4.1.4.2.

173. Gal. *Hipp. 3 Epid.* 3.58, 17a.710K.

174. Procop. *Pers.* 2.22.29.

175. Hp. *Vict.* 1.10, 6.484–86L.

176. Hp. *Epid.* 3.1.1–12, 3.24–44L.

177. Stephanus of Athens, *In Hippocratis Prognosticum commentaria III*, 1.17, 1,2:56. Mercuriale wrote the Greek word διαπήδησις, a term that refers to the transudation of blood through bodily tissue.

178. Mercuriale's lectures on this topic were printed in *Tractatus de maculis pestiferis, de hydrophobia* (Padua: Meietti, 1580).

179. Hp. *Acut.*, 17, (5) 2.60–62L; Stephanus of Athens, *In Hippocratis Prognosticum commentaria III*, 1.17, 1,2:54–56. Mercuriale wrote the Greek word βλητττός here.

180. Hp. *Aph.* 1.1, 4.458L.

181. Plut. *Plat.* 1.1–2, *Moralia*, 999c–1000c; Sex. Emp. *P.* 2.3–7 (14–79). Mercuriale employed the Greek word κριτήρια.

182. [Pseudo] Gal. *Hipp. Hum.* 1.7, 16.81K. The commentary on the Hippocratic treatise *Humors* that once was attributed to Galen is a Renaissance forgery written by Giovanni Battista Rasario. For details of the forgery, see Christina Savino, "Giovanni Battista Rasario and the 1562–63 Edition of Galen. Research, Exchanges and Forgeries," *Early Science and Medicine* 27, no. 4 (2012): 428–37.

183. Thuc. 3.87.

184. Liv. 4.21, 4.25. This plague lasted from 436 to 433 BCE in Livy's telling.

185. Villani, *Cronica*, 1.2, 1:11.

186. The *Provveditori alla Sanità*, or Health Office, was established in Venice in 1486 in response to the plague of 1478.

187. Thuc. 2.51.

188. Villani, *Cronica*, 1.2, 1:10.

189. Evagrius, *Historia ecclesiastica* 4.29; Nicephorus Callistus, *Historia ecclesiastica* 17.18, vol. 147, cols. 265–68.

190. Giovanni Boccaccio, *Decameron*, tr. George H. McWilliam, 2nd ed. (London: Penguin, 1999), first day, introduction, 5–13. Villani, *Cronica*, 1.2, 1:8–15.

191. Thuc. 2.54.

192. Ovid, *Metam.* 7.561–62.

193. Var. *Res rust.* 1.4.4.

194. *Corpus Iuris Civilis* 43.23.1.

195. DL, 8.70.

196. Plut. *Adversus Colotem*, 32, *Moralia*, 1126b.

197. Var. *Res rust.* 1.4.5. Aquilo is a northerly wind.

198. Plin. *NH* 7.50.170.

199. Gal. *Cib.* 1, 6:750–51K; Avenzoar, *Liber theisir*, 39v.

200. Dion. Hal., *Antiquitates romanae* 4.69.2.

201. The Taurian games were a religious festival established in Rome, according to tradition, under the rule of Tarquinius Superbus (d. 495 BCE). *Taurus* means bull in Latin. Sextus Pompeius Festus gave an account of the etymology in agreement with Mercuriale's. See Festus, *De verborum significatione* 18.

202. Vitr. *De archit.* 1.4.1–12. Annibale Raimondo, a Veronese astrologer, believed the plague was caused by drinking from wells contaminated by saltwater. See Raimondo, *Discorso*.

203. Despars, *Fen prima quarti Canonis*, comm. 4.1.4.1, fol. 117r.

204. Sabellico, *Historiae rerum venetarum*, 1060.

205. For the numerous authors who put forward this view with regard to poverty and the plague at Milan and elsewhere, see Cohn, *Cultures of Plague*, 208–37.

206. Plut. *Quaest. Rom.* 94, *Moralia* 286c–d. Aesculapius (Asclepius in Greek) was the Roman god of healing and medicine.

207. Var. *Res rust.* 1.4.5; Plut. *De Iside* 79, *Moralia* 383c–d; Gal. *Ther. Pis.* 16, 14.281K; Aëtius, *Libri medicinales*, ed. Alessandro Olivieri, in *Corpus medicorum graecorum*, vol. 8.2 (Berlin: Academia Litterarum, 1950), 5.95, 81–82.

208. Raymond, *De peste*, 59.

209. Gal. *Ther. Pis.* 16, 14.281K.

210. Diod. Sic. 14.71.

211. In Venice the pesthouse was indicated by the term *lazzaretto* or *lazaretto*, a name for both of the islands in the Venetian lagoon where people and goods were quarantined. The hospital on the Lazzaretto Vecchio was built in 1423. The Lazzaretto Nuovo was established in 1468 and used primarily to examine incoming goods and people and to hold healthy people under quarantine. The sick and the dead were sent to the Lazzaretto Vecchio. For related documents, see David Chambers and Brian Pullan, eds., *Venice: A Documentary History, 1450–1630* (Toronto: University of Toronto Press, 2001), 113–19; Palmer, "Control of Plague," 326–27, 355. The term *lazaretto* has come to refer to pesthouses more generally both in Venice and beyond.

212. Thuc. 2.50.

213. Lucian, *Scyth.* 2.

214. Leviticus 14.1–57.

215. Liv. 3.6. L. Aebutius Helva and P. Servilius Priscus held the consulship in 463 BCE.

216. Sabellico, *Historiae rerum venetarum*, 1060.

217. Hp. *Nat. Hom.* 9, 6.56L.

218. Cels. 1.10.1.

219. Avicenna, *Canon* 1.3.5.1.

220. Avicenna, *Canon* 1.3.5.1.

221. Rhazes, *Liber ad Almansorem*, 4.25, fol. 20r.

222. Averroes, *Colliget libri VII* (Venice: Giunta, 1562), 6.17, fol. 142v. Averroes, or Abū l-Walīd Muḥammad ibn Rušd (1126–1198), was a philosopher, jurist, and physician from Cordoba. He was among the most influential philosophers during the late Middle Ages and Renaissance, especially in the Latin tradition. He was especially known for his commentaries on Aristotle, for which he gained the nickname "The Commentator."

223. Sandalwood was generally understood to be of three different kinds: white, red, or yellow.

224. Averroes recounted Avenzoar's recommendation of goat urine. See Averroes, *Colliget*, 6.17, fol. 142v.

225. Hdn. 1.12.2. Laurentum was a city in ancient Latium, south of Ostia and southwest of Rome.

226. The use of perfumed gloves and balls carried in the hands is described in Benedetti, *Novi avisi di Venetia*, sig. B2v.

227. *Myrtillus* refers probably to *Vaccinium myrtillus*, a plant native to northern Europe that was widely used in German apothecaries.

228. Thphr. *HP* 4.4.2; Athenaeus, *Deipnosophistae* 3.26, 83d–e.

229. Avicenna, *Canon* 1.3.5.1.

230. Plut. *De musica* 42, *Moralia* 1146b–c; Pausanias, *Graeciae descriptio* 1.14.4; Hom. *Il.* 1.472–75.

231. Gal. *Febr. Diff.* 1.6, 7.293–94K.

232. Avicenna, *Canon* 4.1.4.1; 4.1.4.5.

233. Gal. *Simp. Med.* 5.12, 11.743–46K.

234. Avicenna, *Canon* 4.1.4.1; 4.1.4.5.

235. Hp. *Vict.* 2.42, 6.538–40L.

236. Rhazes, *Liber ad Almansorem*, 4.25, fol. 20r.

237. Cels. 1.10.3.

238. Hp. *Acut.* 37, (10) 2.299–300L; Hp. *Vict.* 2.44, 6:542L.

239. Averroes, *Colliget*, 6.17, fol. 142v.

240. Pimpinella probably refers to *Pimpinella saxifraga* (burnet-saxifrage) or to *Pimpinella anisum*.

241. *Omphacium* is oil made from unripe olives.

242. Hp. *Epid.* 2.4.3, 5.126L; Hp. *Epid.* 6.4.11, 5.133L. Ainos is not an island but rather a mountain on the island of Cephalonia.

243. Averroes, *Colliget*, 6.17, fol. 142v.

244. Gal. *Aliment. Fac.* 2.6, 6:569K.

245. Dioscorides, *De materia medica libri quinque*, ed. Max Wellmann (Berlin: Weidmann, 1902), 1.124, 113.

246. Avicenna, *Canon* 2.2.42; 4.6.1.4.

247. Mithridates VI Eupator of Pontus (c. 135–63 BCE) was the king of Pontus and was credited for inventing a recipe for a complex compound medicine that, according to legend, was a universal antidote. Renaissance pharmacies sold versions of the medicine that bore his name.

248. Gal. *Meth. Med.* 12.8, 10.866K.

249. Hor. *Epod.* 3.1–8.

250. This compound (*auripigmentum*) is made from white arsenic (*arsenicum album*) and sulfur. Adrian VI was pope from 1522 to 1523.

251. Gal. *Comp. Med. Gen.* 3.2, 13.568K; Gal. *Simp. Med.* 9.3.4, 12.212K.

252. Manna refers to so-called aerial honey, a sweet residue that famously formed on plants.

253. Niccolò Falcucci, *De medica materia septem sermonum liber [Sermones medicales]* (Venice: Giunta, 1533), 2.4.2.12, 182v. Falcucci (d. 1412) practiced medicine in his native Florence and gained fame for his *Sermones medicales,* a comprehensive work on theoretical and practical medicine.

254. Presumably here Mercuriale was referring to the cloacae of chicken, which were used as a treatment for buboes; see Heinrichs, "Live Chicken Treatment."

255. Oribasius, *Collectionum medicarum reliquiae, libri I–VIII*, ed. J. Raeder, in *Corpus medicorum graecorum*, vol. 6.1.1 (Leipzig and Berlin: Teubner, 1928), 8.24, 271.

256. Moses Maimonides, *Aphorismi* (Basel: Henricpetri, 1579), 9.42, 270.

257. Aëtius, *Libri medicinales*, 5.133, 8.2:108. Herodotus was a physician of the pneumatic school who lived in Rome in the first century CE.

258. *Panatella* is a broth made from marrow and breadcrumbs.

259. Avicenna, *De medicinis cordialibus* (Venice: Giunta, 1562), fol. 563r.

260. *Jallab* is a sweet drink originating from the Middle East traditionally made from carob, dates, grape molasses, and rose water.

261. Gal. *Simp. Med.* 9.1.4, 12.191–92K.

262. Hp. *Epid.* 1.19, (9) 2.658K.

263. Gal. *Febr. Diff.* 1.5, 7.287–89K. Dyscrasia means an imbalanced mixture or temperament.

264. The translation of this sentence follows the Latin of the 1601 edition that adds the word "non" before "convenire."

265. Despars, *Fen prima quarti Canonis*, comm. 4.1.4.2, fol. 118r.

266. These were the ingredients of so-called pills attributed to Rufus that circulated in early modern Europe. Rufus flourished around 100 CE.

267. Simplicius, *In Aristotelis categorias commentarium*, ed. Karl Kalbfleisch, vol. 8 of *Commentaria in Aristotelem graeca* (Berlin: Reimer, 1907), comm. 8, p. 230. Simplicius wrote that he took this information from Arrian.

268. Gal. *Simp. Med.* 9.1.4, 12.191–92K; Gal. *Ther. Pis.* 16, 14.280–82K.

269. Avicenna, *Canon* 4.1.4.4.

270. Hp. *Aph.* 2.29, 4.478L.

271. "Benedicta" compounds were typically made from turbith, scammony, and hermodactyl.

272. Averroes, *Colliget*, 7.31, 167r.

273. Avenzoar, *Liber theisir*, fol. 39v.

274. *Cuscuta epithymum.*

275. A genus of mushrooms.

276. Avicenna, *De medicinis cordialibus*, fol. 562v.

277. This cure is found in Avenzoar, *Liber theisir*, fol. 39r.

278. Avicenna, *Canon* 4.1.4.4.

279. Gal. *Meth. Med.* 4.6, 10.287–89K. Mercuriale wrote the Greek phrase διὰ τὴν κακοηθίαν.

280. [Pseudo] Gal. *Hipp. Hum.* 1.12, 132–33. Aëtius, *Libri medicinales*, 5.133, 8.2:107–8; Avicenna, *Canon* 4.1.4.14; Paulus Aegineta, *Libri I–IV*, ed. Johan L. Heiberg, in *Corpus medicorum graecorum*, vol. 9.1 (Berlin: Teubner, 1921), 2.35, 109. Repletion (*plenitudo*) refers to a fullness of the body with blood. This theory regarding bloodletting is that the amount of blood let should be proportional to the degree of repletion.

281. Gal. *Hipp. Acut. Vict.* 4.17, 15.767K.

282. Gal. *Meth. Med. Glauc.* 1.15, 11.44K.

283. Gal. *Hipp. 1 Epid.* 3.9, 17a.288–89K.

284. Oribasius, *Collectionum medicarum reliquiae*, 7.19, 218.

285. Gal. *Comp. Med. Loc.* 8.4, 13:174K.

286. Oribasius, *Collectionum medicarum reliquiae*, 8.19, 1:266.

287. [Pseudo] Gal. *Hipp. Hum.* 1.14, 16:155K; Moses Maimonides, *Aphorismi*, 8.114, 246.

288. Despars, *Fen prima quarti Canonis*, comm. 4.1.4.3, fol. 123r.

289. This herb refers to a species of ranunculus that was sometimes called "pes corvi" or "crow's foot."

290. Dioscorides, *De materia medica libri quinque*, vol. 1, 2.61, 140; [pseudo] Dioscorides, *Liber de venenis eorumque praecautione et medicatione*, ed. Kurt Sprengel (Leipzig: Knobloch, 1830), 1, 15–17. In the sixteenth century, this work on poisons was widely believed to be by Dioscorides and printed with many translations and commentaries of Dioscorides' *De materia medica*. See John Marion Riddle, "Dioscorides," in *Catalogus translationum et commentariorum*, vol. 4, ed. F. Edward Cranz and Paul Oskar Kristeller (Washington, DC: Catholic University of America Press, 1980), 118–25.

291. Girolamo Mercuriale, *De compositione medicamentorum* (Venice: Giunta, 1590), fols. 103r–4r.

292. Diapalma refers to a plaster or bandage named for the spatula made from a palm branch that was used to stir the mixture.

293. Reading ipsae for ipse.

294. Gal. *Hipp. 2 Epid.* 3.10, 17a.410–11K; Mercuriale's translation of the fragment is found in Galen, *Operum non extantium fragmenta*, vol. 11 of *Omnia quae extant opera* (Venice: Giunta, 1576), fols. 41v–42v. This fragment is also most likely a sixteenth-century forgery by Giovanni Battista Rasario; see Savino, "Giovanni Battista Rasario," 437.

295. Hp. *Morb.* 4.4, (35) 7.548L. See also Hp. *Morb.* 1.15, 6.168L.

296. Hp. *Aph.* 4.55, 4.522L; Gal. *Hipp. Aph.* 4.55, 17b.734K.

297. Hp. *Epid.* 3.9, 3.90L.

298. Hp. *Epid.* 3.4, 3.74L.

299. Gal. *Simp. Med.* 9.1.4, 12.191K.

300. Hp. *De flat.* 6, 6.96–98L.

301. Paulus Aegineta, *Libri I–IV*, 2.34–35, 1:107–9; Aëtius, *Libri medicinales*, 5.133, 8.2:107–10; Avicenna, *Canon* 4.1.4.1–5; Rhazes, *Liber ad Almansorem*, 10,26, fol. 54v.

302. Gal. *Dieb. Decret.* 3.13, 9.939–940K.

303. Hp. *Epid.* 1.24, (11) 2.670–74.

304. Gal. *Hipp. Aph.* 1.7, 17b.374; Gal. *Diff. Resp.* 3.9, 7.935–36K.

305. Gal. *Febr. Diff.* 1.3, 7.281K.

306. Gal. *Simp. Med.* 9.1.4, 12.191K.

307. Hp. *Epid.* 3.4, 3.74L.

308. Diachylon is an unguent made out of plant juices.

309. Egyptian unguent was typically made with verdigris, honey, and red alum.

310. Sarcocolla is a gum resin made from *Atragalus sarcocolla*, a shrub native to Persia.

311. Here, Mercuriale wrote the Greek word ἄνθραξ.

312. Plin. *NH* 26.4.5. Lucius Aemilius Paullus Macedonicus and Quintus Marcius Philippus were elected censors in 164 BCE.

313. Hp. *Epid.* 3.7, 3.84L. Mercuriale wrote in Greek σήψεις.

314. Thuc. 2.49; Eus. *HE* 9.8.1. Eusebius recounted the epidemic that occurred under Maximinus Daia (ruled 305–313). Mercuriale did not address Eusebius' account of the plague that began in 249 CE, found at *HE*, 7.21–22. Nicephorus Callistus, *Historia ecclesiastica*, 7.28, vol. 146, col. 1268.

315. Gal. *Ven. Art. Dissect.* 7, 2.803K.

316. Eus. *HE* 9.8.1. It seems Mercuriale was referring to the revised translation of Eusebius that reads: "Morbi etiam cuiusdam novi & peregrini (exulceratio quaedam erat, quae aestus & fervoris proprio nomine anthrax, id est carbunculus appellatur) gravis & violenta impressio," found at Eusebius, *Historiae ecclesiasticae scriptores graeci*, ed. John Christopherson and Joannes Curterius (Paris: Frémy, 1571), 199. The translation made by Rufinus (c. 345–410) differs significantly and does not contain the words "novi" and "peregrini" for this passage. See Eusebius, *Ecclesiastica hystoria* (Lyon: Giunta, 1526), fol. 73r.

317. Averroes, *Colliget*, fols. 166r–67v.

318. Gal. *Meth. Med.* 14.12, 10.984–85K; Avicenna, *Canon* 4.3.1.18.

319. Andron's lozenge was compounded with gall, myrrh, alum, pomegranate seeds, vinegar, and wine, among other ingredients.

320. Apostles' unguent was made according to various recipes that typically contained alum, myrrh, mastic, rose oil, and terebinth.

321. Hp. *Aph.* 7.87, 4.608L.

322. Plin. *NH* 36.69.203.

323. Rhazes, *Liber ad Almansorem*, 7.10, fol. 31v.

# BIBLIOGRAPHY

## PRIMARY SOURCES

Aëtius. *Libri medicinales*, ed. Alessandro Olivieri. Vol. 8.2 of *Corpus medicorum graecorum*. Berlin: Academia Litterarum, 1950.

Agricola, Georg. *De peste libri tres*. Basel: Froben, 1554.

Albertus Magnus. *De animalibus libri XXVI*, ed. Hermann Stadler. 2 vols. Münster: Aschendorff, 1916–1921.

Albucasis. *Liber theoricae nec non practicae*. Augsburg: Grimm, Sigmund & Wirsung, 1519.

Alderotti, Taddeo. *Expositiones in divinum pronosticorum Ipocratis librum*. Venice: Giunta, 1527.

Altomare, Donato Antonio. *De medendis febribus ars medica*. Venice: De Maria, 1562.

Aristotle. *Problematum Aristotelis sectiones duaedequadraginta*, trans. Theodore Gaza. Lyon: Mirallietum, 1550.

Avenzoar. *Liber theisir* in *Colliget Averrois . . . Theizir Abynzoar morbos omnes*. Venice: Scoto, 1542.

Averroes. *Colliget libri VII*. Venice: Giunta, 1562.

Avicenna. *De medicinis cordialibus*. Venice: Giunta, 1562.

———. *Metaphysica, sive eius prima philosophia*. Venice: Scoto, 1495.

Basil. *Homilia in Psalmum primum*. Vol. 29 of *Patrologiae cursus completus: Series graeca*, ed. J.-P. Migne. Paris: Migne, 1857.

Benedetti, Rocco. *Novi avisi di Venetia ne' quali si contengono tutti i casi miserabili, che in quella al tempo della peste sono occorsi*. Urbino: Benacci, 1577.

Boccaccio, Giovanni. *Decameron*, trans. George H. McWilliam. 2nd ed. London: Penguin, 1999.

Bonagente, Vittorio. *Decem problemata de peste*. Venice: Valgrisi, 1556.

Brahe, Tycho. *De nova et nullius aevi memoria prius visa stella*. Copenhagen: Laurentius Benedictus, 1573.

Canobbio, Alessandro. *Il successo della peste occorsa in Padova l'anno MDLXXVI*. Venice: Perchacino, 1577.

Capriolo, Elia. *Chronica de rebus Brixianorum*. Brescia: Arundi, 1505.

Cortusi, Guglielmo. *De novitatibus Padue et Lombardie*. Vol. 12 of *Rerum italicarum scriptores*, ed. Lodovico Antonio Muratori. Milan: Società Palatina, 1728.

Cyprianus. *De mortalitate*. Vol. 4 of *Patrologiae cursus completus: Series latina*, ed. J.-P. Migne. Paris: Migne, 1844.

Del Garbo, Tommaso. *Consiglio contr'alla peste*. Venice: Giunta, 1556.

Despars, Jacques. *Fen prima quarti Canonis Avicennae principis cum explanatione Jacobi de Partibus*. Lyon: Lascaris, 1498.

Dioscorides. *De materia medica libri quinque*, ed. Max Wellmann. 2 vols. Berlin: Weidmann, 1902–1907.

*Ecclesiasticae historiae.* Paris: Estienne, 1544.

Eusebius. *Ecclesiastica hystoria.* Lyon: Giunta, 1526.

———. *Historiae ecclesiasticae scriptores graeci*, ed. John Christopherson and Joannes Curterius. Paris: Frémy, 1571.

Falcucci, Niccolò. *De medica materia septem sermonum liber [Sermones medicales].* Venice: Giunta, 1533.

Falloppio, Gabriele. *Opuscula.* Padua: Bertelli, 1566.

Fernel, Jean. *On the Hidden Causes of Things*, ed. and trans. John M. Forrester. Leiden: Brill, 2005.

Ficino, Marsilio. *Il consiglio contra la pestilentia.* Venice: Giunta, 1556.

Fioravanti, Leonardo. *Del regimento della peste.* Venice: Ravenoldo, 1565.

Fracastoro, Girolamo. *De sympathia et antipathia rerum liber unus. De contagione et contagiosis morbis et curatione libri III.* Venice: Giunta, 1546.

———. *La dottrina fracastoriana del contagium vivum*, ed. Francesco Pellegrini. Verona: Valdonega, 1950.

Galen. *Claudii Galeni Opera omnia*, ed. Karl Gottlob Kühn. 20 vols. Leipzig: Knobloch, 1821–1833.

———. *Operum non extantium fragmenta.* Vol. 11 of *Omnia quae extant opera.* Venice: Giunta, 1576.

Gentile da Foligno. *De febribus. Expositio in prima fen quarti Canonis Avicennae.* Venice: Giunta, 1526.

Godfrey of Viterbo. *Pantheon sive Universitatis libri, qui chronici appellantur, XX.* Basel: Parcus, 1559.

Gratiolo, Andrea. *Discorso di peste.* Venice: Polo, 1576.

Gregory of Nyssa. *De pauperis amandis oratio II.* Vol. 46 of *Patrologiae cursus completus: Series graeca*, ed. J.-P. Migne. Paris: Migne, 1863.

Hippocrates. *Oeuvres complètes d'Hippocrate*, ed. Emile Littré. 10 vols. Paris: Baillière, 1839–1861.

Ingrassia, Giovanni Filippo. *Informatione del pestifero, et contagioso morbo.* Palermo: Mayda, 1576.

Lando, Bassiano. *De origine et causa pestis patavinae, anni 1555.* Venice: Griffio, 1555.

Maimonides, Moses. *Aphorismi.* Basel: Henricpetri, 1579.

Manfredi, Girolamo. *Tractato de la pestilentia/Tractatus de peste*, ed. Tommaso Duranti. Bologna: CLUEB, 2008.

Massa, Niccolò. *Ragionamento sopra le infermità, che vengono dall'aere pestilentiale del presente anno.* Venice: Ziletti, 1556.

Mattioli, Pier Andrea. *Commentarii, in libros sex Pedacii Dioscoridis Anazarbei, De medica materia.* Venice: Valgrisi, 1554.

Mercuriale, Girolamo. *Censura operum Hippocratis* in *Hippocratis Coi opera quae extant graece et latine*, ed. G. Mercuriale. Venice: Giunta, 1588.

———. *De compositione medicamentorum.* Venice: Giunta, 1590.

———. *De morbis cutaneis et omnibus corporis humani excrementis.* Venice: Meietti, 1572.

———. *De pestilentia.* Padua: Meietti, 1577.

———. *De venenis et morbus venenosis tractatus.* Padua: Meietti, 1584.

———. *Medicina practica.* Frankfurt: Schönwetter, 1602.

———. *Praelectiones pisanae in epidemicas Hippocratis historias.* Venice: Giunta, 1597.

———. *Tractatus de maculis pestiferis, de hydrophobia.* Padua: Meietti, 1580.

———. *Variarum lectionum libri quatuor.* Venice: Meietti, 1570.

Morosini, Andrea. *Degl'istorici delle cose veneziane quali hanno scritto per pubblico decreto*, vol. 6. Venice: Lovisa, 1719.

Nicephorus Callistus Xanthopulus. *Breviarum.* Vol. 100 of *Patrologiae cursus completus: Series graeca*, ed. J.-P. Migne. Paris: Migne, 1865.

———. *Historia ecclesiastica*, Vol. 147 of *Patrologiae cursus completus: Series graeca*, ed. J.-P. Migne. Paris: Migne, 1865.

Oribasius. *Collectionum medicarum reliquiae, libri I–VIII*, ed. J. Raeder. Vol 6.1.1 of *Corpus medicorum graecorum*. Leipzig: Teubner, 1928.

Paulus Aegineta. *Libri I–IV*, ed. Johan L. Heiberg. Vol. 9.1 of *Corpus medicorum graecorum*. Berlin: Teubner, 1921.

Platina. *Historia de vitis pontificum Romanorum*. Venice: Tramezzino, 1562.

[Pseudo] Alexander of Aphrodisias. *Problemata physica*. Vol. 1 of *Physici et medici graeci minores*, ed. Julius L. Ideler. Berlin: Reimer, 1841.

[Pseudo] Dioscorides. *Liber de venenis eorumque praecautione et medicatione*, ed. Kurt Sprengel. Leipzig: Knobloch, 1830.

[Pseudo] Mesue. *Opera*. Venice: Giunta, 1570.

Raimondo, Annibale. *Discorso nel quale chiaramente si conosce la viva et vera cagione, che ha generato le fiere infermità*. Padua: s.n., 1576.

Raymond Chalin de Vinario. *De peste libri tres*, ed. Jacques Dalechamps. Lyon: Rouillé, 1552.

Rhazes. *Liber ad Almansorem*. Venice: De Leuco, 1508.

Sabellico, Marco Antonio. *Historiae rerum venetarum ab urbe condita libri XXXIII*. Basel: Episcopius, 1556.

Simplicius. *In Aristotelis categorias commentarium*, ed. Karl Kalbfleisch. Vol. 8 of *Commentaria in Aristotelem graeca*, ed. Hermann Diels. Berlin: Reimer, 1907.

———. *In Aristotelis physicorum libros quattuor priores commentaria*. Vol. 9 of *Commentaria in Aristotelem graeca*, ed. Hermann Diels. Berlin: Reimer, 1882.

Stephanus of Athens. *In Hippocratis Prognosticum commentaria III,* ed. and trans. John M. Duffy. Vol. 11.1.2 of *Corpus medicorum graecorum*. Berlin: Akademie-Verlag, 1983.

Themistius. *Paraphrasis,* trans. Ermolao Barbaro. Venice: Scoto, 1559.

Theophanes. *Chronographia*. Vol. 108 of *Patrologiae cursus completus: Series graeca*, ed. J.-P. Migne. Paris: Migne, 1863.

Villani, Matteo. *Cronica. Con la continuazione di Filippo Villani*, ed. Giuseppe Porta. Parma: Fondazione Pietro Bembo, U. Guanda, 1995.

Zacco, Girolamo. *Theoremata ex variis naturalis philosophiae, ac medicinae locis deprompta per Hieronymum Zaccum patavinum disputanda*. Padua: Pasquato, 1573.

## SECONDARY SOURCES

Arrizabalaga, Jon. "Facing the Black Death: Perceptions and Reactions of University Medical Practitioners." In *Practical Medicine: Salerno to the Black Death*, ed. Luis García Ballester et al., 237–88. Cambridge: Cambridge University Press, 1994.

Barry, John M. "The Single Most Important Lesson from the 1918 Influenza," *New York Times*, March 17, 2020, https://www.nytimes.com/2020/03/17/opinion/coronavirus-1918-spanish -flu.html (accessed October 1, 2020).

Beloch, Karl Julius. *Storia della popolazione d'Italia*, trans. Marco Nardi. Florence: Le Lettere, 1994.

Benedictow, Ole J. *The Black Death 1346–1353: The Complete History*. Woodbridge: Boydell, 2004.

Bylebyl, Jerome L. "The School of Padua: Humanistic Medicine in the Sixteenth Century." In *Health, Medicine and Mortality in the Sixteenth Century*, ed. Charles Webster, 335–70. Cambridge: Cambridge University Press, 1979.

Campbell, Anna Montgomery. *The Black Death and Men of Learning*. New York: Columbia University Press, 1931.

Cavallo, Sandra, and Tessa Storey. *Healthy Living in Renaissance Italy*. Oxford: Oxford University Press, 2013.

Cerasoli, Giancarlo, and Brunella Garavini. "Il codice di Girolamo Mercuriale con le annotazioni sulle condizioni climatiche di Padova nel 1577–1578 durante la peste (BCR, Cod. 467)," *Ravenna studi e ricerche* 11, no. 2 (2004): 131–51.

Chambers, David, and Brian Pullan, eds. *Venice: A Documentary History, 1450–1630*. Toronto: University of Toronto Press, 2001.

Cohn, Samuel K., Jr. "The Black Death: End of a Paradigm," *American Historical Review* 107, no. 3 (2002): 703–38.

———. *Cultures of Plague: Medical Thinking at the End of the Renaissance*. Oxford: Oxford University Press, 2010.

Crawshaw, Jane L. Stevens. *Plague Hospitals: Public Health for the City in Early Modern Venice*. Burlington, VT: Ashgate, 2012.

Croke, Brian. "Procopius, from Manuscripts to Books: 1400–1850," *Histos* supplement 9 (2019): 1.1–173.

Deer Richardson, Linda. "The Generation of Disease: Occult Causes and Diseases of the Total Substance." In *The Medical Renaissance of the Sixteenth Century*, ed. Andrew Wear et al., 175–94. Cambridge: Cambridge University Press, 1985.

De Vivo, Filippo. "Pharmacies as Centres of Communication in Early Modern Venice," *Renaissance Studies* 21, no. 4 (2007): 505–21.

Duncan-Jones, R. P. "The Antonine Plague Revisited," *Arctos* 52 (2018): 41–72.

Durling, Richard J. "A Chronological Census of Renaissance Editions and Translations of Galen," *Journal of the Warburg and Courtauld Institutes* 24, no. 3–4 (1961): 230–305.

———. "Girolamo Mercuriale's *De modo studendi*," *Osiris* 2nd ser. 6 (1990): 181–95.

Eisenberg, Merle, and Lee Mordechai, "The Justinianic Plague and Global Pandemics: The Making of the Plague Concept," *American Historical Review* 125, no. 5 (2020): 1632–67.

Fenlon, Iain Alexander. *The Ceremonial City: History, Memory and Myth in Renaissance Venice*. New Haven, CT: Yale University Press, 2008.

Fortuna, Stefania. "Girolamo Mercuriale editore di Galeno." In *Girolamo Mercuriale, medicina e cultura nell'Europa del Cinquecento*, ed. Alessandro Arcangeli and Vivian Nutton, 217–31. Florence: Olschki, 2008.

Giard, Luce. "Histoire de l'université et histoire du savoir: Padoue (XIVe–XVIe siècle)," *Revue de synthèse* 104 (1983): 139–69.

Grafton, Anthony. *What Was History? The Art of History in Early Modern Europe*. Cambridge: Cambridge University Press, 2007.

Green, Monica H. "Taking 'Pandemic' Seriously: Making the Black Death Global," *Medieval Globe* 1 (2014): 27–61.

Harper, Kyle. "Pandemics and Passages to Late Antiquity: Rethinking the Plague of c. 249–270 Described by Cyprian," *Journal of Roman Archaeology* 28 (2015): 223–60.

Hasse, Dag Nikolaus. *Success and Suppression: Arabic Sciences and Philosophy in the Renaissance*. Cambridge, MA: Harvard University Press, 2016.

Heinrichs, Erik. "The Live Chicken Treatment for Buboes," *Bulletin of the History of Medicine* 91, no. 2 (2017): 210–32.

Henderson, John. "The Invisible Enemy: Fighting the Plague in Early Modern Italy," *Centaurus* 62, no. 2 (2020): 263–74.

Hirai, Hiro. *Le concept de semence dans les théories de la matière à la Renaissance*. Turnhout: Brepols, 2005.

Honigsbaum, Mark. "Revisiting the 1957 and 1968 Influenza Pandemics," *Lancet* 395, no. 10240 (2020): 1824–26.

Jones, Colin. "Plague and Its Metaphors in Early Modern France," *Representations* 53 (Winter 1996): 97–127.

Jones, David S. "COVID-19, History, and Humility," *Centaurus* 62, no. 2 (2020): 370–80.

Jouanna, Jacques. "Air, Miasma, and Contagion in the Time of Hippocrates and the Survival of Miasmas in Post-Hippocratic Medicine (Rufus of Ephesus, Galen and Palladius)." In *Greek Medicine from Hippocrates to Galen: Selected Papers*, 121–36. Leiden: Brill, 2012.

———. "Mercuriale, commentateur et éditeur d'Hippocrate." In *Girolamo Mercuriale, medicina e cultura nell'Europa del Cinquecento*, ed. Alessandro Arcangeli and Vivian Nutton, 269–300. Florence: Olschki, 2008.

Keiser, George, R. "Two Medieval Plague Treatises and Their Afterlife in Early Modern England," *Journal of the History of Medicine and Allied Sciences* 58, no. 3 (2003): 292–324.

Konstantinidou, Katerina, et al. "Venetian Rule and Control of Plague Epidemics on the Ionian Islands during the 17th and 18th Centuries," *Emerging Infectious Diseases* 15, no. 1 (2009): 39–43.

Lane, Frederic C. *Venice: A Maritime Republic*. Baltimore: Johns Hopkins University Press, 1975.

Little, Lester K. "Plague Historians in Lab Coats," *Past & Present* 213, no. 1 (2011): 267–90.

Lohr, Charles H. *Latin Aristotle Commentaries. Volume II Renaissance Authors*. Florence: Olschki, 1988.

Lonie, Iain M. "The 'Paris Hippocratics': Teaching and Research in Paris in the Second Half of the Sixteenth Century." In *The Medical Renaissance of the Sixteenth Century*, ed. Roger K. French et al., 155–74. Cambridge: Cambridge University Press, 1985.

Maloney, Gilles, and Raymond Savoie. *Cinq cent ans de bibliographie hippocratique, 1473–1982*. Saint-Jean Chrysostome, Quebec: Editions du Sphinx, 1982.

Marcus, Hannah. "What the Plague Can Teach Us about the Coronavirus," *New York Times,* March 1, 2020, https://www.nytimes.com/2020/03/01/opinion/coronavirus-italy.html (accessed October 1, 2020).

Martin, Craig. *Renaissance Meteorology: Pomponazzi to Descartes*. Baltimore: Johns Hopkins University Press, 2011.

———. *Subverting Aristotle: Religion, History, and Philosophy in Early Modern Science*. Baltimore: Johns Hopkins University Press, 2014.

Martin, John Jeffries. *Venice's Hidden Enemies: Italian Heretics in a Renaissance City*. Berkeley: University of California Press, 1993.

McCormick, Michael. "Rats, Communications, and Plague: Toward an Ecological History," *Journal of Interdisciplinary History* 34, no. 1 (2003): 1–25.

Monfasani, John, "The Pseudo-Aristotelian *Problemata* and Aristotle's *De animalibus* in the Renaissance." In *Natural Particulars: Nature and the Disciplines in Renaissance Europe*, ed. Anthony Grafton and Nancy Siraisi, 205–47. Cambridge, MA: MIT Press 1999.

Nockels Fabbri, Christiane. "Treating Medieval Plague: The Wonderful Virtues of Theriac," *Early Science and Medicine* 12, no. 3 (2007): 247–83.

Nutton, Vivian, "Greek Science in the Sixteenth-Century Renaissance." In *Renaissance and Revolution: Humanists, Scholars, Craftsmen, and Natural Philosophers in Early Modern Europe*, ed. J. V. Field and Frank A. J. L. James, 15–28. Cambridge: Cambridge University Press, 1993.

———. "The Reception of Fracastoro's Theory of Contagion," *Osiris* 2nd ser. 6 (1990): 196–234.

———. "The Rise of Medical Humanism: Ferrara, 1464–1555," *Renaissance Studies* 11, no. 1 (1997): 2–19.

———. "With Benefit of Hindsight: Girolamo Mercuriale and Simone Simoni on Plague," *Medicina e storia* 11 (2006): 5–19.

Ogilvie, Brian W. *The Science of Describing: Natural History in Renaissance Europe.* Chicago: University of Chicago Press, 2006.

Ongaro, Giuseppe. "Girolamo Mercuriale." In *Dizionario biografico degli Italiani*, 73:620–25. Rome: Istituto della Enciclopedia Italiana, 2009.

Ongaro, Giuseppe, and Elda Martellozzo Forin. "Girolamo Mercuriale e lo Studio di Padova." In *Girolamo Mercuriale, medicina e cultura nell'Europa del Cinquecento*, ed. Alessandro Arcangeli and Vivian Nutton, 29–50. Florence: Olschki, 2008.

Pade, Marianne. "Thucydides." In *Catalogus translationum et commentariorum*, ed. Virginia Brown, 8:103–81. Washington, DC: Catholic University of America Press, 2003.

Palmer, Ada. *Reading Lucretius in the Renaissance.* Cambridge, MA: Harvard University Press, 2014.

Palmer, Richard. "The Control of Plague in Venice and Northern Italy." PhD diss., University of Kent at Canterbury, 1978.

———. "Girolamo Mercuriale and the Plague of Venice." In *Girolamo Mercuriale, medicina e cultura nell'Europa del Cinquecento*, ed. Alessandro Arcangeli and Vivian Nutton, 51–65. Florence: Olschki, 2008.

———. "Pharmacy in the Republic of Venice in the Sixteenth Century." In *The Medical Renaissance of the Sixteenth Century*, ed. Andrew Wear et al., 100–117. Cambridge: Cambridge University Press, 1985.

Pennuto, Concetta. "Girolamo Mercuriale e la dottrina dei giorni critici." In *Girolamo Mercuriale, medicina e cultura nell'Europa del Cinquecento*, ed. Alessandro Arcangeli and Vivian Nutton, 301–17. Florence: Olschki, 2008.

———. *Simpatia, fantasia e contagio: Il pensiero medico e il pensiero filosofico di Girolamo Fracastoro.* Rome: Edizioni di Storia e Letteratura, 2008.

Pomata, Gianna. "*Praxis Historialis:* The Uses of *Historia* in Early Modern Medicine." In *Historia: Empiricism and Erudition in Early Modern Europe*, ed. Gianna Pomata and Nancy G. Siraisi, 105–46. Cambridge, MA: MIT Press, 2005.

Preti, Cesare. "Giovanni Filippo Ingrassia." In *Dizionario biografico degli Italiani*, 62:396–99. Rome: Istituto della Enciclopedia Italiana, 2004.

Preto, Paolo. *Peste e società a Venezia nel 1576.* Venice: Neri Pozza, 1978.

Pugliano, Valentina. "Pharmacy, Testing, and the Language of Truth in Renaissance Italy," *Bulletin of the History of Medicine* 91, no. 2 (2017): 233–73.

Riddle, John Marion. "Dioscorides." In *Catalogus translationum et commentariorum*, ed. F. Edward Cranz and Paul Oskar Kristeller, 4:1–144. Washington, DC: Catholic University of America Press, 1980.

Ruderman, David B. "Out of the Mouths of Babes and Sucklings." In *Monsters and Monstrosity in Jewish History: From the Middle Ages to Modernity*, ed. Iris Idelson-Shein and Christian Wiese, 213–28. London: Bloomsbury, 2019.

Ruisinger, Marion Maria. "Die Pestarztmaske im Deutschen Medizinhistorischen Museum Ingolstadt." *NTM Zeitschrift für Geschichte der Wissenschaft, Technik und Medizin* 28 (June 2020): 235–52.

Savino, Christina. "Giovanni Battista Rasario and the 1562–63 Edition of Galen. Research, Exchanges and Forgeries," *Early Science and Medicine* 27, no. 4 (2012): 413–45.

Seitz, Jonathan. *Witchcraft and Inquisition in Early Modern Venice*. Cambridge: Cambridge University Press, 2011.

Siraisi, Nancy G. *Avicenna in Renaissance Italy: The Canon and Medical Teaching in Italian Universities after 1500*. Princeton, NJ: Princeton University Press, 1987.

———. "History, Antiquarianism, and Medicine: The Case of Girolamo Mercuriale," *Journal of the History of Ideas* 64, no. 2 (2003): 231–51.

———. *History, Medicine, and the Traditions of Renaissance Learning*. Ann Arbor: University of Michigan Press, 2007.

———. "*Medicina Practica*: Girolamo Mercuriale as Teacher and Textbook Author." In *Scholarly Knowledge: Textbooks in Early Modern Europe*, ed. Emidio Campi et al., 287–305. Geneva: Droz, 2008.

Stathakopoulos, Dionysios. "Crime and Punishment: The Plague in the Byzantine Empire, 541–749." In *Plague and the End of Antiquity: The Pandemic of 541–749*, ed. Lester K. Little, 99–118. Cambridge: Cambridge University Press, 2007.

Turner, David. "The Politics of Despair: The Plague of 746–747 and Iconoclasm in the Byzantine Empire," *Annual of the British School at Athens* 85 (1990): 419–34.

Vagenheim, Ginette. "Una collaborazione tra antiquario ed erudito: I disegni e le epigrafi di Pirro Ligorio nel *De arte gymnastica* di Girolamo Mercuriale." In *Girolamo Mercuriale, medicina e cultura nell'Europa del Cinquecento*, ed. Alessandro Arcangeli and Vivian Nutton, 127–57. Florence: Olschki, 2008.

Watts, Edward. "What Rome Learned from the Deadly Antonine Plague of 165 A.D.," *Smithsonian Magazine*, April 28, 2020, https://www.smithsonianmag.com/history/what-rome-learned-deadly-antonine-plague-165-d-180974758/ (accessed October 1, 2020).

Weiner, Gordon M. "The Demographic Effects of the Venetian Plagues of 1575–77 and 1630–31," *Genus* 26, no. 1/2 (1970): 41–57.

Ziegler, Michelle. "The Black Death and the Future of the Plague," *Medieval Globe* 1 (2014): 259–83.

# INDEX

Acron of Acragas, 81
Aesculapius, temple of, 80–81, 132n206
Aëtius, 9, 81, 94, 100, 106
Agricola, Georg, 4
Agrigento, 79
Ainos, 38, 89
air: and contagion, 16, 35, 54, 56, 58–61, 67–68, 71; as cause of plague, 10–11, 14–15, 22, 29, 38–39, 47, 50, 69–70, 74–75, 110; as compound body, 43–44; breathing of, 17, 48, 61, 67–68, 83, 88; constitution of, 12, 19, 44–46, 63; corruption of, 12–13, 43, 64, 79–79, 80; healthy, 80–81, 85; improvement of, 19, 81, 85–87, 93; in past plagues, 49–50; in Venice and Padua, 39–41, 46–47, 50, 62; poisoning of, 66
Albertus Magnus, 57, 130n125
Albucasis, 9, 57, 130n126
Alderotti, Taddeo, 44–45, 128n74
Al-Rāzī. *See* Rhazes
Altomare, Donato Antonio, 38, 41–42
Al-Zahrawi. *See* Albucasis
Ammianus Marcellinus, 42, 45
anatomy, 2, 8
animals, 9, 13, 81–82; and poison, 43, 66; as agents of transmission, 5, 6, 56; as food, 89; as signs, 9, 39–40, 62–64; death during plagues, 15, 31, 49
anthrax. *See* carbuncle
Antonine plague, 4–5, 14–15, 21, 40, 49, 65, 69. *See also* Galen
Apollo, 42, 45
Apollonius of Tyana, 39
Apollonius, physician, 102
Appian of Alexandria, 60
Archigenes, 103, 106
Aristotle, 12, 13, 52, 66, 80; *History of Animals*, 31; *Meteorology*, 43; on contagion 15, 34–36, 51–52; on occult qualities, 42, 45; *On the*

*Generation of Animals*, 42, 45; *On the Length and Shortness of Life*, 43; *Problems*, 8, 34–35, 43, 45–46, 51
Armenian bole, 42, 95–96, 106, 112, 115, 127n60; in recipes, 90, 99
Arrian, 96
Asia, 18, 111
astrology, 4, 14, 40, 42
Athenaeus, 87
Athenian plague, 4–5, 9, 15, 65, 78; duration, 76; mortality during, 31, 49; overcrowding, 69, 83; symptoms, 77, 111
Athens, 32
atomism, 9, 41–42
Auster. *See* wind
Austria, 36, 86
Avenzoar, 9, 38, 45, 79, 86, 97, 126n43
Averroes, 9, 85–86, 89, 97, 111, 133n222
Avicenna, 34, 57, 72, 126n22; as authority, 9–10, 12; *Metaphysics*, 38; on bodily dispositions, 47–48, 69; on celestial powers, 45, 70; on cures for plague, 88, 90, 95, 97–98, 100, 112; on occult qualities, 42, 44–45, 47; *On the Powers of the Heart*, 95; on thick air, 84–85; prevention of plague, 85, 88
Avidius Cassius, 42
Avignon, 68

Babylonia, 42
Basil the Great, 33
bathing, 9, 80, 88
Black Death, 5–6, 15, 21, 49, 65–66, 69, 76–77
Black people, 66
blood, 31, 72–73; snake's, 112
bloodletting, 7, 18–19, 23, 97, 100–102. *See also* cupping; surgery
Boccaccio, Giovanni, 77
Boncompagni, Giacomo, 27, 125n2
Botanic Garden. *See* Orto Botanico

poisons, 57; in air, 43, 62, 66; in contagion, 50–54, 56–58, 60, 66; treatments for, 18, 90, 92–93, 95–98, 100–5, 108–12; within the body, 10, 13, 37–38, 48–49, 54–55, 57, 62, 71–74
Polybus, 42, 127n61
poor, the, 23, 31, 79–80, 83–84
Porcacchi, Tommaso, 83
Porro, Girolamo, 83
Portugal, 23
preternatural: disease, 51, 107–8; heat, 13, 18, 37, 43, 52–53, 55, 71; symptoms, 31, 51
Procopius, 4, 34–35, 40, 49, 73
*Provveditori alla Sanità. See* Health Office
Publius Servilius Priscus, 83, 133n215
purge, 18, 77, 90, 92–93, 95–98, 108, 111–13
putrefaction, 10, 12; absence in plague victims, 55, 71; and fevers, 38, 71–72, 96, 106; cause of, 13; in plague, 37, 42–43, 52–53, 59, 79, 89, 100, 110; in spontaneous generation, 40; of air, 42–43, 81, 84–85; treatments for, 17–19, 87, 89, 92–95, 109, 112

quarantine, 1, 6–7, 17, 22–23, 82–83, 117
Quintus Marcius Philippus, 110, 136n312

rabies, 57, 62, 66
rain, 41, 46–46, 64
Raymond Chalin De Vinario, 4, 68, 81
regimen, 17, 42, 93, 111
Rhazes, 9, 48, 85, 89, 106, 113
Rome, 1, 27, 61; plagues in, 42, 45, 49, 71, 76, 83, 86
Rufinus, 111, 136n316
Rufus of Ephesus, 93–94, 96, 134n266

Sabellico, Marco Antonio, 49, 80, 84, 129n106
Sacchi, Bartolomeo. *See* Platina
seeds of disease, 9–10, 16, 31–34, 58–59, 63, 69
Selinunte, 79
Seneca, 67
Sextus Empiricus, 74
Sicily, 1, 6, 11, 36, 40, 46, 77, 127n52
simples. *See* medications
Simplicius, 96, 125n5, 134n267
sleep, 17, 87, 93, 111
smallpox, 14
Sparta, 88
Speroni, Sperone, 27, 125n3

spirit, 42; bodily, 47, 55, 71–72, 94; inhaled, 51–52, 60–61
Stephanus of Athens, 44–45, 73–74
Sun, 46, 61, 110
supernova, 14, 127n49
surgery, 17–18, 93, 100–104, 107, 111, 118. *See also* bloodletting; cautery; cupping
sympathy, 10, 16, 54
symptoms, 5, 10–11, 14, 38, 40, 105–6, 111; in Venice and Padua, 6–7, 31, 33, 50, 70–74, 77; relief of, 93, 124n79. *See also* preternatural
syphilis. *See* French disease
syrup, 18, 92, 98

Tacitus, 61
temperament, 12, 14–15, 17, 48, 54, 118; ideal, 13, 39; of the brain, 72, of the heart, 71, 96, of the seasons, 46
Thales, 88
Themistius, 28, 125n5
Theophanes the Confessor, 129n109
Theophrastus, 57, 64, 87
theriac, 18, 42, 96–97, 118, 124n79, 127n60; in recipes, 90–91, 99
Thucydides, 9, 31, 40, 49, 65, 76–78, 111; on contagion, 33, 81–82; translations of, 4. *See also* Athenian plague
Toxaris, 82
Transylvania, 36, 77
Trent, 6, 40, 46, 77; as origin of plague, 23, 31, 62, 69
Treviso, 62, 65
Trincavelli, Vittore, 2
true plague, 6–8, 11, 14–15, 33, 36–38, 41–42, 45–47
tumor. *See* buboes; carbuncles

Uganda, 5
Ulpian, 78–79
University of Bologna, 2, 20, 27
urine, 31, 71–73, 105–6, 111; as cure, 42, 49–50, 96; goat's, 86

Valla, Lorenzo, 4
vapors, 17, 46, 84–85; from bodies, 16, 51–53, 56, 66; in contagion, 53–55, 57–61, 67, 71, 87; of the dead, 80–81; terrestrial, 13, 38–39, 42–43, 87; within bodies, 72, 103, 105. *See also* air; miasmas; spirits

# ACKNOWLEDGMENTS

I am grateful to the many people who helped me with this book. I thank Alex Bamji for the conversation we had in Venice that prompted me to think about Mercuriale. Gideon Manning helped revise and correct the introduction. Hannah Marcus tracked down difficult-to-obtain material for me. Silvia Marchiori solved several problems and gave me much appreciated feedback. James Naus helped me grasp better Byzantine sources. I benefitted from conversations with David Gentilcore and Marco Sgarbi. The reviewers' reports greatly improved the work. One of the reviewers, Cindy Klestinec, identified herself to me. Her enthusiasm for the project is greatly appreciated. Nancy Hirschmann gave me many valuable suggestions. Noreen O'Connor-Abel and Jill Twist saved me from many errors and inconsistencies. The book would not have been possible without Jerry Singerman's efforts and guidance. I thank all my Latin teachers over the years, including Joann Arthur, Dennis Hughes, Ed Phillips, and Joseph Cummings. Università Ca' Foscari Venezia's *fondo di primo insediamento* supported me materially. Most of all, Chiara Bariviera supported the project in countless ways, from the smallest details to the conception of the project as a whole.